Artists of Alberta

Artists
of Alberta

Suzanne Devonshire Baker

The University of Alberta Press

First published by
The University of Alberta Press
Edmonton, Alberta, Canada 1980

ISBN 0-88864-067-6
Copyright © The University of Alberta Press 1980

Canadian Cataloguing in Publication Data

Baker, Suzanne Devonshire.
    Artists of Alberta

    ISBN 0-88864-067-6

    1. Artists—Alberta.   2. Art—Alberta.
    I. Title.
    N6546.A4B34   709′.7123   C79-091225-2

Design by John Luckhurst
Warren Clark Graphic Design

Printed by
Hignell Printing Limited
Winnipeg, Manitoba

Contents

Jury statements

Harry Savage

On viewing the works that were submitted for the first edition of *Artists of Alberta*, I was surprised at the number of artists that reside in Alberta and was visually enthused with the variety of works and the quality of the art that is being created in this province. I think this book will prove useful to artists, art dealers, and serious collectors.

Norman Yates

The task of selecting a limited number of names to be represented in this first edition of *Artists of Alberta* was a formidable one. To some degree, the problem was relieved through the editor's proposal to not only invite four jurors but also to draw them from different sections of the province.

Each of the members employed their awareness of art production and their sensitivity to its quality as sincerely and as carefully as possible. In spite of this effort, there will be concern about artists who may have been missed in this survey. Since it is my understanding that a second volume may be produced, oversights will be corrected and the number of artists increased.

Art in Alberta is in a state of flourishing expansion, with many forms and styles emerging in this exciting part of our development. This information on some of the artists who are currently residing in Alberta is a first step in the provision of access to the artists and the works they are producing in the province.

Stan Perrott

It has often been stated that significant visual art reflects the society and geography in which and from which it forms itself. That cliché seems underscored by the work of Alberta artists presented to, and selected by, the jury for inclusion in this book.

The diversity of the province's mountains, plains, badlands, and bush, its monuments of sandstone, steel, and glass, its evangelists, oil barons, and bronc riders—all these factors and more may suggest the phenomenon of parochial regionalism. On the contrary, the evidence indicates that our artists are reaching into an almost limitless range of creative possibilities. Local isolation has been relieved by influences from the "world scene" through travel, importation of exhibitions, immediate media communication, and the inflow of art instructors to colleges and universities. No single "ism," theme, technique, or content can presently bring Alberta art into focus for definition. While there is lacking what is traditionally referred to as maturity, there is more to be experienced in the ferment of curiosity, testing, and evaluation.

Although the task has been to select works of quality, however difficult to define, it has been important to arrive at a comprehensive survey rather than an appeal to elitist taste for international style. The appointed jury brought together the widest possible scope of artistic philosophies. What might have been a difficult impasse turned into a most suitable reflection of the variety marking art in this province.

To prophesy the future of Alberta art would be as foolish as trying to predict the capricious weather of the area. Presently, we are witnessing the healthy vigour of a rapidly expanding art community bringing refreshing concepts to public attention. Before long, another publication may be necessary to mark the progress, the independence, and the individualism that may characterize Alberta art.

Ron Moppett

Power, prestige, and the accumulation of personal wealth were my reasons for becoming an art critic, of course. In those days Alberta politicians rose and fell at my whim. One night, in a fit of pique, I denounced a senior cabinet minister's taste in ceramics. The next morning he was sitting in the back benches, never again to hold ministerial office. A critic's life was busy, busy, busy.

Two full-time secretaries were appointed to look after my social obligations. On one of the high points—the papal tour of Canada's West—His Holiness commented on my discreet use of Florentine marble in my living-room. Speaking of my home: let me finally lay the so-called Affaire de Moppett to rest. I was not "given" the former Government House by the then wife of the then premier; I bought it. For one dollar. The price may seem low, but the place needed work.

Yes, Alberta was good to me. Particularly good in 1980, later to be called The Year of the Ninety-five. It may seem a little naughty of me, but I like to think I created those artists.

"Money cannot make Art!" screamed number ninety-six, pushing his way in for a personal audience after hearing of his rejection. But it can influence it, I thought a few days later, as I read the penniless wretch's obituary. (Perhaps we should have included him in a footnote. Those three watercolours I bought from the widow were quite passable.)

That's the problem with selection, however: some make it, some don't. I wonder what did happen to Perrott, Yates, and Savage. Not bad chaps—in their field.

From *Confessions of an Art Critic: The Formative Years (1945-1985)*. University of Panama Press, 1997.

Introduction

The artists now working in Alberta have revealed a wide and exciting variety of style, technique, media, and concept. Although Alberta has a relatively young visual arts community, it has been stimulated by several sources. The growth and influence of art education institutions throughout the province and the influx of instructors from many parts of the world, as well as the development of art exhibition centres through which valuable exhibitions are made available to the public, have contributed greatly to the growth of the art community in the past decade.

There are no predominant unifying regional similarities apparent in the work of the artists represented in this book. The diversity and range of experimentation and process in visual art being produced in this province is exciting. It is even more exciting to realize that there are so many artists producing such high calibre work.

Obviously, it was impossible to represent all the visual artists in Alberta in this publication. I know that there are many deserving artists, including those who are well known, as well as younger artists who, perhaps, were not actively involved with the art community when selection took place, whose work is not found in these pages. I hope that a subsequent edition will include the work of these artists.

The selection committee consisted of four artists, two from the northern portion of the province and two from the south. Ron Moppett and Stan Perrott are from Calgary while Harry Savage and Norman Yates are from Edmonton. Their work differs widely in process and philosophy. They have all acted as jurors in all aspects of the visual arts on many occasions, although this is the first time they have been on the same selection committee. Their knowledge and diverse experience has proved invaluable, and I would like to thank them for the care and concern they brought to the task. It was not an easy one. All four members of the committee are deservedly represented in this book and the decision to include them was mine.

Much of the art reproduced here will be familiar to those who have watched the development of the art community in Alberta over the years. However, a provision was made for those artists who had recently graduated or who were just beginning their artistic careers, and almost one-quarter of the book is devoted to them. Further selection was based on several criteria. All the artists had to be working, producing, and contributing, through exhibitions or in other ways, to the Alberta visual art community, and all must have been residents of the province for a minimum of five years. A range of media and technique was taken into consideration so as to provide as comprehensive a survey as possible. Due to space and budget limitations, photography could not be included in this edition.

The time between selection and publication allowed for documentation of the art work to be reproduced and for research. Some of the artists may have begun to work in different directions or in different media. It is most likely, too, that their work will continue to change. Innovation and growth are essential elements in the creative process.

Most of the artists themselves chose the work they would like to have included here. It is important to note that although only one piece could be photographed for this book many of these artists are working in or experimenting with several media, and not only the media of the work by which they are represented.

The factual information contained on these pages reveals the variety of productivity and philosophies of contemporary Alberta artists. Lists of exhibitions, grants, and awards, no matter how pedantic, serve to illustrate that many artists in Alberta are exhibiting, competing, and marketing their work across Canada and often throughout the world.

It has been an exciting and stimulating project for me and the attempt has been to produce a valid and comprehensive survey of visual art and artists in the province of Alberta. I am very grateful to Alberta Culture for their assistance in helping me with research costs and to those corporations and individuals who are assisting the publication costs. Also, I would like to thank Linda Wedman for her keen and helpful work on portions of this publication.

Suzanne Devonshire Baker

Doug Haynes

Doug Haynes, Chairman of the Department of Art and Design, the University of Alberta, Edmonton, graduated from the Provincial Institute of Technology and Art (Alberta College of Art), Calgary, 1958. In 1970 Haynes became an Associate of the Royal Canadian Academy.

He was awarded an Alberta Visual Arts Board Scholarship in 1958 and a Netherlands Government Scholarship to study in Holland from 1960 to 1961. Other awards include a Canada Council Senior Arts Award, 1967; an All-Alberta Purchase Award, 1969; and a City of Edmonton Creative Arts Award, 1975. His work has been acquired for permanent collections such as the Alberta Art Foundation, Edmonton; the Canada Council Art Bank, Ottawa, Ontario; and civic galleries in Edmonton, Charlottetown, Prince Edward Island, and London, Ontario. He has been represented in many major exhibitions across Canada, including *Abstraction West—Emma Lake and After*, the National Art Gallery, Ottawa, Ontario, 1975; *Vision '77*, Banff, Alberta, 1977; *Certain Traditions*, the Edmonton Art Gallery, Edmonton, 1978; and *Seven Prairie Painters*, the Art Gallery of Ontario, Toronto, Ontario, 1979. He has held several solo exhibitions, the most recent of which were at Red Deer College, Red Deer, Alberta, 1977; Gallery One, Toronto, Ontario, 1978; and the Downstairs Gallery, Edmonton, 1979.

In the early 1970s Haynes was concerned with landscape content in his paintings. His works were produced on unstretched canvas, and while exploring the surface qualities produced through the acrylic medium his emphasis or preoccupation was on content and statement. The paintings he has produced in the last five years display an emphasis on the formal properties of colour, shape, and line. He is less concerned with content or a message and is more spontaneous in his approach. Colour is more vibrant, and the canvases are large.

Doug Haynes can be reached through the University of Alberta, Department of Art and Design, or at 5, 15104 Stony Plain Road, Edmonton, Alberta.

Title and date Canadian Loyalist 1977
Medium acrylic on canvas
Size 170.7 cm x 133.5 cm

Walter Drohan

Born in Calgary in 1932, Walter Drohan graduated from the Alberta College of Art, Calgary, in 1956. Post-graduate study was done at the Cranbrook Academy of Art, Michigan, in 1957. He is an instructor and supervisor at the Alberta College of Art, Calgary.

Drohan received a Canada Council grant in 1968 for study in Germany, and his work is housed in the Alberta Art Foundation, Edmonton; Government of Canada Federal Building, Wetaskiwin, Alberta; and private collections throughout the province. Walter Drohan was elected to the Royal Canadian Academy in 1976 and

has served on the executive of the Alberta Potters Association as well as on several juries for ceramic exhibitions. One-person shows were held at the Edmonton Art Gallery, Edmonton, 1974; the University of Saskatchewan, Regina, Saskatchewan, 1975; and Mount Royal College, Calgary, 1976. Drohan has completed commissions for the Government of Alberta, the Government of Canada, and several corporations in the province. Group shows include *The History of Ceramics in Alberta,* the Edmonton Art Gallery, Edmonton, 1975, and *Fibre, Clay, Metal,* the Alberta College of Art, Calgary, 1976, as well as numerous local shows.

Drohan's major concern, at present, is with large-scale canvases of landscape or elements in landscape. However, he has also been involved with the ceramic process for the last twenty years. His latest clay work, mainly in porcelain, has been evolving with more pictorial emphasis, with Drohan utilizing techniques of drawing and painting on the surface of the works. He has had a long-standing preoccupation with drawing and painting airplanes. Research into the heraldry and mechanical details is undertaken prior to the execution of each work.

He can be reached at Box 112, Cochrane, Alberta.

Title and date 03U - 6 1976
Medium oil on canvas
Size 108.5 cm x 131.5 cm

George Mihalcheon

Born in Vegreville, Alberta, George Mihalcheon graduated from the Alberta College of Art, Calgary. He was employed for several years as an artist and art director for advertising agencies and has been an instructor at the Alberta College of Art since 1960, where he is supervisor of foundation and core programs.

Mihalcheon is represented in the collections of the Fathers of Confederation Gallery, Charlottetown, Prince Edward Island; the University of Calgary; the Students' Union Collection, the University of Alberta, Edmonton; the Southern Alberta Institute of Technology, Calgary; the Alberta Art Foundation, Edmonton; and corporate collections in Edmonton and Calgary. Mihalcheon has exhibited nationally and was included in *9 out of 10, A Survey of Canadian Art*, Hamilton Art Gallery, Hamilton, Ontario, 1974, and the *Alberta Art Foundation Premiere Exhibition*, European tour, 1975. He has participated in a two-person show at the Griffith Gallery, Vancouver, 1972; in Alberta College of Art staff shows; and in annual exhibitions held by the Alberta Society of Artists.

For the past several years Mihalcheon has been working with collage. The non-objective imagery is created with shapes cut out of pre-painted acrylic canvas and applied to a stretched canvas ground. Colour is a dominant factor in his collage works. He often applies paint with an airbrush, and the imagery is based upon "man-made symbols imposed on nature."

Mihalcheon can be reached through the Alberta College of Art, 1301-16 Avenue NW, Calgary, Alberta, or at his home at 23 Cambridge Road NW, Calgary, Alberta.

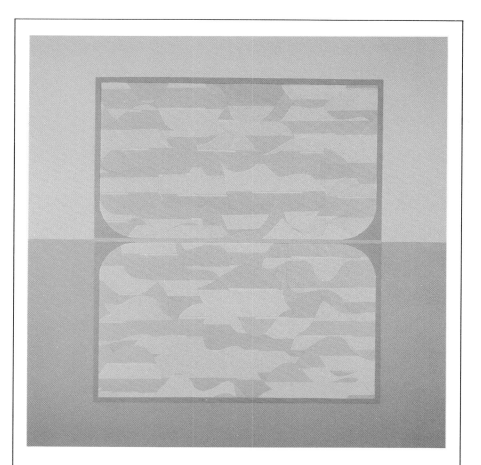

Title and date Tangerine 1973
Medium acrylic on canvas
Size 153 cm x 154 cm

Hazel Litzgus

Hazel Litzgus was born in Lloydminster, Alberta, in 1927. She works in Calgary and is represented in the collection of the Alberta Art Foundation, Edmonton.

Litzgus has held a one-person show at the Allied Art Centre, Calgary, and has participated in two two-person shows at Canadian Art Galleries in Calgary. She was also included in *Peoples Art*, the National Gallery of Canada, Ottawa, and the *Alberta Art Foundation Premiere Exhibition*, European travelling tour, 1975-76.

Litzgus paints in watercolour and considers herself to be a primitive artist. Her direct and naive approach to painting has developed into a distinctive style. Subject matter is taken from memories of her childhood on a small Alberta farm. Themes such as the school dance, harvesting, and family gatherings document rural life in Alberta. The size of her work is usually small, at the most measuring 59 cm x 69 cm.

She can be reached at her home address of 14 Columbia Place NW, Calgary, Alberta.

Title and date The Christmas Oranges 1975
Medium watercolour
Size 32.5 cm x 42 cm

Rick Chenier

Born in Edmonton in 1945, Rick Chenier graduated with a Bachelor of Fine Arts from the University of Alberta in 1969 and a Master of Visual Arts from the University of Alberta in 1972. Chenier is currently an assistant professor with the Department of Art and Design, University of Alberta, Edmonton.

His paintings are included in the collections of the Edmonton Art Gallery, Edmonton; the Alberta Art Foundation, Edmonton; and the University of Alberta, Edmonton. Chenier has held solo shows at the Edmonton Art Gallery, Edmonton, 1974; Latitude 53 Gallery, Edmonton, 1976; and the Edmonton Art Gallery, Edmonton, 1977. He began exhibiting in 1971 and has participated in several major group shows, including *Nine Out of Ten—A Survey of Canadian Painting*, Art Gallery of Hamilton, Hamilton, Ontario, 1975; *Prairies—Western Canadian Painting*, Saidye Bronfman Centre, Montreal, Quebec, 1974; and *Prairie '74*, the Edmonton Art Gallery, Edmonton, 1974.

Chenier works with acrylic on canvas. Since 1976 he has been using a diamond-shaped format which he considers as a container or an arena for optical movement caused by the confrontation between large, poured, or brushed shapes against a loosely stained ground. The grounds are usually pale in colour, contrasting with the more vivid markings and painterly strokes which float across the surface. These loose shapes are further emphasized by their containment in the strictly defined diamond-shaped field. The scale of his work is generally large.

Rick Chenier's studio address is 302 Tower Building, 10135-103 Street, Edmonton, Alberta.

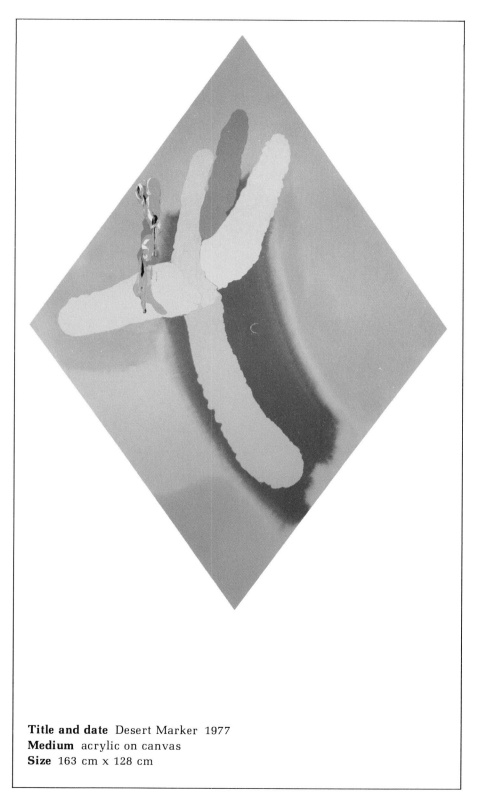

Title and date Desert Marker 1977
Medium acrylic on canvas
Size 163 cm x 128 cm

Joice Hall

Joice Hall was born in Edmonton in 1943. She studied at the Alberta College of Art, Calgary, between 1961 and 1965.

Hall is represented in the permanent collections of the following art galleries and museums: the University of Calgary; the Canada Council Art Bank, Ottawa, Ontario; the Alberta Art Foundation, Edmonton; the Mendel Art Gallery, Saskatoon, Saskatchewan; and private collections in Canada and the United States. Hall exhibits nationally and has shown in numerous group exhibitions, including *Eight Calgary Artists*, the Mendel Art Gallery, Saskatoon, Saskatchewan, 1976; *Painting Now*, the Agnes Etherington Art Gallery, Kingston, Ontario, 1977; *Albertawork*, the University of Calgary and the Alberta College of Art, Calgary, 1977; *Realist Painters in Calgary*, Subway Gallery, Calgary, 1978; *Calgary Artists*, invitational, Peter Whyte Gallery, Banff, Alberta, 1979.

For the last few years Hall has been working on a series of large, irregularly shaped canvases based on landscape imagery and incorporating various symbols. These fantasy paintings, titled *Celebration Landscapes*, are moving toward more complex imagery as the series develops. "They are landscape ideas that function allegorically, as they are descriptions of one thing (conjugal union) under the image of another (natural landscape); the penis becomes a tree; the vagina, a flower; bedclothes become hills; colour, shape, and emotion combine to create a feeling of ecstasy for growth in nature and growth in human love."

Joice Hall can be reached at 19 Rosetree Road NW, Calgary, Alberta.

Title and date Dream Garden, Celebration Landscape no. 8 1977
Medium oil on canvas
Size 235 cm x 206 cm

Jim Brodie

Jim Brodie was born in Hamilton, Ontario, in 1946 and was educated at Concordia University, Montreal, Quebec; Sheridan College, School of Visual Arts, Oakville, Ontario; and Central Washington State College, Ellensburg, Washington, where he received a Master of Arts in printmaking and art history. Brodie has been an instructor at the Alberta College of Art, Calgary, since 1973.

He has received several awards, including an Alberta Culture Project Cost Grant, 1978, and purchase awards in *14th Annual Calgary Graphics*, Calgary, 1974; *5th City of Hamilton Annual*, Hamilton, Ontario, 1974; and *101st Ontario Society of Artists Annual*, 1972. His work can be found in the collection of the Alberta Art Foundation, Edmonton; the National Gallery of Canada, Ottawa; the Art Gallery of Hamilton, Hamilton, Ontario; the Art Gallery of Toronto, Toronto, Ontario; Grant MacEwan Community College, Edmonton; and corporate and university collections in Canada and Australia. Solo and small group exhibitions have been held at Civic Gallery, Rotorua, New Zealand, 1980; the Cultural Centre, Burlington, Ontario, 1980; Whitehorse Public Library, Yukon, 1979; Royal Melbourne Institute of Technology, Australia, 1978; the University of Calgary, 1977; and Otaco Gallery, Ellensburg, Washington, 1977.

Brodie's work is often a combination of printmaking techniques and may include serigraphy, lithography, intaglio, and collography. All works are on paper and all involve a photographic process at some stage in their development. Brodie is mainly concerned with the positive and negative attitudes in his socio-cultural matrix, especially toward violence, native peoples, and the exploitation of the province of Alberta by industry.

Jim Brodie may be contacted through the Alberta College of Art, 1301-16 Avenue NW, Calgary, Alberta, or at his home at 806-23 Avenue NW, Calgary, Alberta.

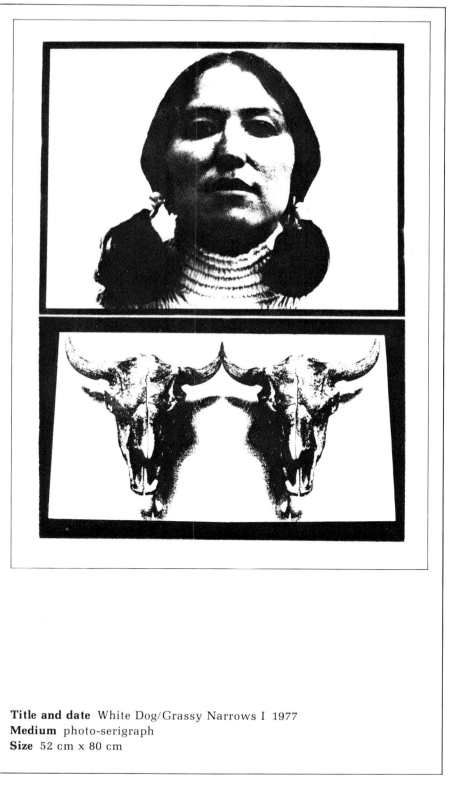

Title and date White Dog/Grassy Narrows I 1977
Medium photo-serigraph
Size 52 cm x 80 cm

Jim Westergard

Jim Westergard was born in Ogden, Utah, in 1939. He graduated with a Bachelor of Fine Arts, 1967, and a Master of Fine Arts, 1969, from Utah State University, Salt Lake City, Utah. Westergard has taught at several art institutions in the United States and has been on staff at Red Deer College, Red Deer, since 1975.

Collections containing his work are the College of Siskiyous, Weed, California; the Art Gallery of Brant, Brantford, Ontario; the Alberta Art Foundation, Edmonton; the Canada Council Art Bank, Ottawa; and the University of Calgary. His exhibitions include *Graphex 4*, the Art Gallery of Brant, Brantford, Ontario, 1976; *Invitational of 4 Alberta Artists*, the University of Liverpool, Liverpool, England, 1977; *Albertawork*, the University of Calgary and the Alberta College of Art, Calgary, 1977; the *Alberta Society of Artists Annual Exhibition*, the Glenbow-Alberta Institute, Calgary, 1977 and 1979; and *Alberta Artists at the Canadian Consulate*, Boston, Massachusetts, 1978.

The imagery in Westergard's drawings develops from the juxtaposition of the double meanings of certain words and the images those meanings provoke, as well as from the juxtaposition of objects which are commonly not associated with each other. The illusion of surfaces, materials, and low relief plays an important role in the work. Colour is built up with layers of coloured pencil applied on the paper like dry washes until the desired colour and value have been achieved. The titles of the drawings, whether developed first or last, are very much a part of the work and add to the humorous content.

Jim Westergard can be reached at 14 Munro Crescent, Red Deer, Alberta.

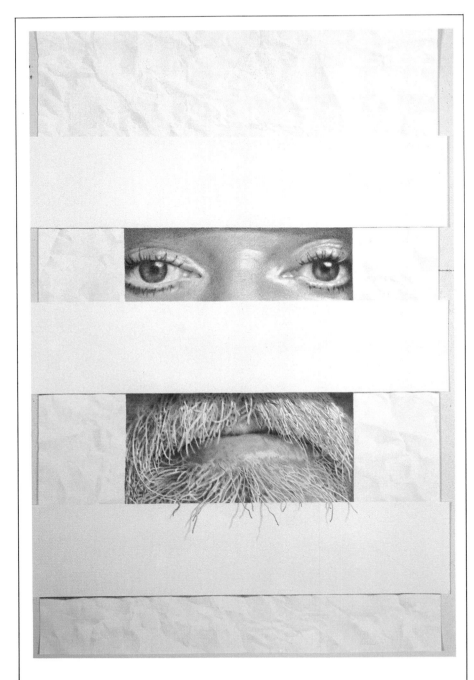

Title and date Sprouts 1977
Medium coloured pencil on paper
Size 86.36 cm x 55.88 cm

Doug Barry

Doug Barry was born in Edmonton, Alberta, 1923. He graduated from the Ontario College of Art, Toronto, Ontario, 1949. Since his graduation Barry has taught with the Department of Fine Arts and the Faculty of Extension at the University of Alberta. He has also taught summer sessions within the province of Alberta, the Yukon, and the Northwest Territories.

His work can be found in the permanent collections of Alberta Culture, Edmonton; the Alberta Art Foundation, Edmonton; Government House, Edmonton; and the Edmonton Art Gallery, Edmonton; and several major

corporations in Alberta. Barry has also completed portraits and murals for public buildings, including fifteen painted panels for Our Lady of the Angels Church, Fort Saskatchewan, Alberta, 1964; a relief cast wall and sculptured altar for St. Anthony's Church, Edmonton, 1965; and the Frank Oliver Bronze Plaque, for the City of Edmonton, 1968. One-person exhibitions were held at the Edmonton Art Gallery, Edmonton, 1974, and Strathcona Place, Edmonton, 1977. Since 1949 Barry has participated in over thirty group exhibitions, including *Art in Alberta, Paul Kane to the Present,* Edmonton Art Gallery, Edmonton, 1973; the *Alberta RCMP; Cen-*

tury Exhibition, touring show, 1974; *Alberta Painters,* Latitude 53 Gallery, Edmonton, 1975; *Barry/Whitehouse,* Latitude 53 Gallery, Edmonton, 1977; and *Alberta Collects Alberta,* Beaver House Gallery, Edmonton, 1979.

Barry's subject matter or theme is mainly that of landscape, and he works on a variable format. He paints on location with oil and watercolour and in his studio with acrylic stains. His main interest lies with the experimentation and control of surface.

Barry can be reached through the mail at Box 6, Site 16, R.R.2, Sherwood Park, Alberta.

Title and date Road to Dorothy #2 1977
Medium acrylic stain on canvas
Size 61 cm x 91 cm

Peter Deacon

Peter Deacon was born in England, 1945. He received a Bachelor of Fine Arts degree from Portsmouth College of Art, England, 1967; an art teacher's diploma from the University of Wales, School of Art Education, Cardiff, Wales, 1968; and a Master of Fine Arts from the Slade School of Art, University College, University of London, England, 1970. He has held lecturing positions in college and art institutions in England and is now an instructor with the Department of Art, University of Calgary.

Deacon has been awarded several scholarships and awards, including prizes at the *Second British International Drawing Biennale*, Middlesborough, England, 1975, and at *Graphex 6*, the Art Gallery of Brant, Brantford, Ontario, 1977. His work is represented in public and private collections in Great Britain, the United States, and Italy, as well as in the Canada Council Art Bank, Ottawa, and the University of Calgary Art Gallery. Deacon has frequently held solo shows at such galleries as the Alberta College of Art Gallery, Calgary, 1974, and Thomas Gallery, Winnipeg, 1977 and 1978. He has also participated in numerous group shows, including *Making Marks*, Norman Mackenzie Gallery, Regina, Saskatchewan, 1977; *Drawings by 12 Canadian Artists*, Thomas Gallery, Winnipeg, Manitoba, 1978; *Graphex 7*, the Art Gallery of Brant, Brantford, Ontario, 1979; and *Alberta Artists*, Artcore Gallery, Vancouver, British Columbia, 1979. He also held a two-person exhibition Deacon/Hushlak, Glenbow-Alberta Institute, Calgary, 1978.

Deacon produces both paintings and drawings. His drawings are done on a paper format of either fifty-five centimetres square or 55 cm x 70 cm, and he produces approximately fifty per year. His paintings range in scale from sixty centimetres square to 182 centimetres square. As well as rollers, Deacon utilizes airbrush and handbrush techniques in his painting process. Both his drawings and his paintings are tightly controlled combinations of geometric and organic imagery. His most recent work emphasizes surface, with bright arrowheads of colour shooting across the composition.

Peter Deacon can be reached through the Department of Art, Faculty of Fine Arts, the University of Calgary, or at his home address of 2414-16 Street SW, Calgary, Alberta.

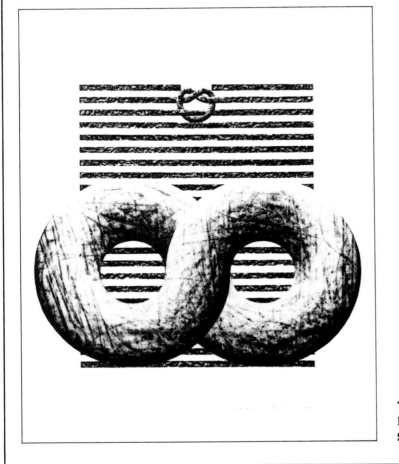

Title and date Twist #11 1977
Medium graphite on paper
Size 70 cm x 55 cm

Raymond St. Arnaud

Edmontonian Ray St. Arnaud was born in 1942 and graduated from the University of Alberta, Edmonton, with a Bachelor of Arts in 1963 and a Bachelor of Arts in fine art and psychology in 1975. From 1968 to 1970 he attended the Northern Alberta Institute of Technology, Edmonton, to study photography. Ray St. Arnaud has taught many photographic workshops. From 1972 to 1974 he was employed by Grant MacEwan Community College, Continuing Education Division, Edmonton, as a colour printing instructor.

His photographs may be found in the permanent collection of the National Film Board, Stills Division, Ottawa, Ontario. One-person shows include the Banff Centre School of Fine Arts, Banff, 1970; the Visual Arts Branch Circulating Show, Department of Culture, Government of Alberta, 1970-71; and Latitude 53 Gallery, Edmonton, 1976 and 1978.

During the last five years of Ray St. Arnaud's career he has been concerned primarily with landscape photography. He began to paint exclusively in 1975, and his imagery is now based on what St. Arnaud labels as "the distortion of reality" as presented by the media, particularly in advertising. His use of artificial colour reflects the "alienation of the individual from itself and society." Acrylic paint is applied on large flat areas of canvas with an airbrush.

St. Arnaud's studio is at 300, Tower Building, 10135-103 Street, Edmonton, Alberta, and he can be reached through the mail at 11232-100 Avenue, Edmonton, Alberta.

Title and date Memories of a Two-Wheeled Carriage 1977
Medium acrylic on canvas
Size 95 cm x 75.75 cm

Clyde McConnell

Clyde McConnell was born in 1944 in Los Angeles, California. He received a Bachelor of Arts from the University of California, Santa Barbara, California, 1966, and a Master of Arts from the University of California, Davis, California, 1968. He is currently on staff at the University of Calgary, and he has taught at the University of California, Sierra College, and at the University of Saskatchewan.

McConnell has received a University of Calgary Research Grant, 1972, and a Canada Council Aid to Galleries Grant, 1975. His work may be found in the collections of Sierra College, Rocklin, California; the University of California, Santa Barbara, California; the Glenbow-Alberta Institute, Calgary; the Alberta Art Foundation, Edmonton; and the Canada Council Art Bank, Ottawa, Ontario. Since 1971, when he became a resident of Alberta, McConnell has exhibited regularly in the province and across Canada. He has held solo exhibitions at the Glenbow-Alberta Institute, Calgary, 1975; Clouds & Water Gallery, Calgary, 1975; Dalhousie University, Halifax, Nova Scotia, 1975; the University of Toronto, Ontario, 1976; the Southern Alberta Art Gallery, Lethbridge, 1979; and the University of California, Davis, California, 1979.

McConnell is interested in photography, drawing, printmaking, and painting. His long association with photography familiarized him with the dye transfer process which was developed several decades ago as a method of making colour photographs. McConnell has adapted this method for use as a printmaking medium. The method is similar to that used in photolithography except that a halftone dot pattern is not necessary and the printing plate is a hardened gelatin film instead of metal or stone.

McConnell's home and studio is at 38 Dalton Bay NW, Calgary, Alberta, or through the Department of Fine Arts, University of Calgary, Calgary, Alberta.

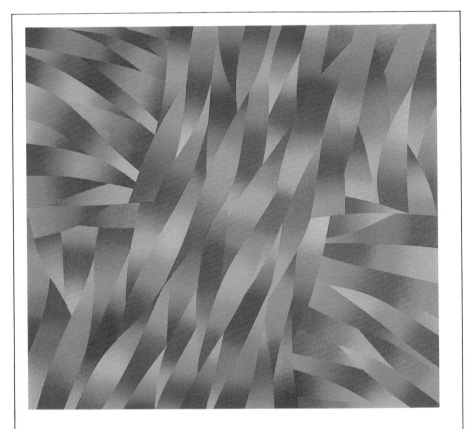

Title and date untitled 1979
Medium acrylic on canvas
Size 45 cm x 45 cm

Isabel Levesque

Born and raised in Castor, Alberta, Isabel Levesque completed her schooling at the Alberta College of Art, Calgary, and the University of Calgary. She furthered her education through courses at the University of Alberta, Edmonton, and the Banff Centre School of Fine Arts.

Permanent collections containing her work include the Alberta Art Foundation, Edmonton; Alberta Culture, Edmonton; and several corporations in Alberta. The Government of Alberta purchased seven of her paintings to be used as gifts on trade missions to Japan, and some of her paintings have been featured on the covers of regional periodicals. Her landscapes are well known to Edmontonians, as she primarily exhibits in that vicinity.

Isabel Levesque uses both acrylic and watercolour to depict the rural landscape of Alberta in all its moods and seasons. Whenever possible her paintings or sketches are made on location, and the subject matter often dictates her choice of media. When painting in watercolour she uses a detailed dry-brush technique. Acrylics are thinly applied, often in glazes. Levesque has no desire to make social comments on her work. "I don't feel that it is necessary to do something that has never been done before; I simply wish to express the pleasure I have with our Alberta countryside. I hope that those who view my paintings will feel the peace, the quiet, and, perhaps, the nostalgia that such an environment brings to me."

Levesque can be contacted at 9536-155 Street, Edmonton, Alberta.

Title and date April Snowfall 1977
Medium acrylic on panel board
Size 46 cm x 61 cm

Barbara Zeigler-Sungur

Barbara Zeigler-Sungur was born in London, Ontario, in 1949. She graduated with a Master of Fine Arts from the University of Illinois, Champaign-Urbana, Illinois. She also attended the Akademie der bildenden Künste (Art Academy), Munich, Germany, and the Universität München (University of Munich).

Permanent collections housing Zeigler-Sungur's prints are the Ontario Arts Council, Toronto, Ontario; Government House, Edmonton; Canada Council Art Bank, Ottawa, Ontario; the Art Gallery of Ontario, Toronto, Ontario; and civic galleries in Oshawa, Sudbury, Grimsby, Guelph, and Brantford, Ontario. She has exhibited widely in national and international print and drawing juried competitions and received an honorarium in *Exhibit 1*, Ontario Arts Council, Toronto, Ontario, 1974; the Special Effects Purchase Award, in the *Student Photography Competition*, the University of Illinois, 1975; the People's Prize, in the *Art Association of Newport 64th Annual American Competition*, Newport, Rhode Island, 1975; and a purchase award in *Graphex 5*, the Art Gallery of Brant, Brantford, Ontario, 1977. Zeigler-Sungur held a one-woman show at the Edmonton Public Library Art Gallery, Edmonton, 1976, and has participated in two-person shows at the Levis Faculty Center, University of Illinois, 1975, and Gallery Pascal, Toronto, Ontario, 1977.

For the past seven years Zeigler-Sungur has been working primarily in the media of printmaking and drawing. Her imagery originates from the collaging of fragments of everyday experience in an unusual and often surrealistic manner. In many works she incorporates a variety of printmaking processes such as lithography, serigraphy, and intaglio.

Barbara Zeigler-Sungur can be reached c/o 10738-123 Street, Edmonton, Alberta.

Title and date Don't Close Your Eyes 1977
Medium lithography and silk-screen
Size 51 cm x 46 cm

Tommie Gallie

Nova-Scotian born Tommie Gallie received his Bachelor of Fine Arts from the Nova Scotia College of Art and Design, Halifax, in 1971. In 1973 he was awarded a Master of Visual Arts degree from the University of Alberta, Edmonton, and he studied at the Banff Centre School of Fine Arts, 1973.

Recent awards include Crestview Foundation Scholarship, 1973; Alberta Cultural Assistance Award, 1973; and a Canada Council Project Grant, 1974. His work may be found in many permanent collections, including the Alberta Art Foundation, Edmonton; the Canada Council Art Bank, Ottawa, Ontario; the Canadian Art Archives, Vancouver, British Columbia; the Government of Alberta Collection, Edmonton; Dalhousie University, Halifax, Nova Scotia; and the University of Alberta, Edmonton. Gallie has exhibited extensively throughout Alberta and has recently held solo shows at the Edmonton Art Gallery, Edmonton, 1975, and the Southern Alberta Art Gallery, Lethbridge, 1976. Two one-person exhibitions were *Hendrik Bres/Tommie Gallie,* Latitude 53 Gallery, Edmonton, 1975, and *Tommie Gallie/Ranjan Sen,* the Glenbow-Alberta Institute Art Gallery, Calgary, 1975. He has participated in many group shows, including *03 23 03*, Institut D'Art Contemporaire, Montreal, Quebec, 1977; *New Abstract Art*, the Edmonton Art Gallery, Edmonton, 1977; *Sculpture on the Prairies*, the Winnipeg Art Gallery, Winnipeg, Manitoba, 1977; *Sculpture Today/Canada*, Ontario Place, Toronto, Ontario, and Hirshhorn Museum, Washington, D.C., 1978; and *Paper Tigers*, circulating tour, 1978 to 1980.

Gallie's sculptures are constructions of both hard and soft woods. Concerned with dynamic and aggressive juxtaposition of form and space, he utilizes the natural characteristics of wood to enhance linear form. These wood constructions range in size from small pieces approximately sixty-one centimetres high to large structures of 153 cm x 365 cm.

Tommie Gallie lives at 10964-84 Avenue, Edmonton, Alberta.

Title and date Stanton 1976
Medium untreated spruce
Size 237.5 cm x 62.5 cm x 157.5 cm

Ann Clarke

B orn in Norwich, England, in 1944, Ann Clarke has been living in Alberta since 1968. She graduated from the Slade School of Fine Arts, the University of London, in England. She has held teaching positions at the University of Alberta, Edmonton; the Nova Scotia College of Art and Design, Halifax, Nova Scotia; the Banff Centre School of Fine Arts, Banff, Alberta; and Red Deer College, Red Deer.

She received the Slade Painting Prize from the University of London in 1966. Other awards include the Government of Alberta Major Cultural Award, 1974, and Canada Council awards in 1973, 1976, and 1978. Clarke has work in public collections in Canada, England, and Australia, including the Queensland Art Gallery, Brisbane, Australia, and the Canada Council Art Bank, Ottawa, Ontario. Solo exhibitions in the last five years have been held at the Edmonton Art Gallery, Edmonton, 1977; the Southern Alberta Art Gallery, Lethbridge, 1979; Hett Gallery, Edmonton, 1980; and Gallery One, Toronto, 1980. Clarke's work was also shown in the *Manisphere International Juried Show*, Winnipeg, Manitoba, 1977; *Certain Traditions*, Edmonton Art Gallery, Edmonton, 1978; *Seven Prairie Painters*, Art Gallery of Ontario, Toronto, Ontario, 1979; and *Three Painters—Haynes, Christie, Clarke*, Gallery One, Toronto, Ontario, 1979.

Ann Clarke usually paints with acrylic on canvas. Her paintings are usually quite large and, as well as acrylic paint, are combinations of a variety of media, including coloured chalk, pastels, charcoal, and a collage technique. Her small work is on paper and also includes a mixture of media. Formal emphasis in her work is on line, colour, and surface.

Ann Clarke lives at 8107-149 Street, Edmonton, Alberta.

Title and date Sea See Shore Sure 1977
Medium acrylic on canvas
Size 160.5 cm x 81.5 cm

Diane Whitehouse

Diane Whitehouse was born in Birmingham, England, in 1940. She received her education at the Birmingham College of Art, Birmingham, England, and Bergen Künsthaverskole, Bergen, Norway.

In 1977 she received a scholarship from the Government of Alberta. She was elected to the Alberta Art Foundation Review Committee in 1976. Collections containing Whitehouse's paintings are Alberta Government House, Edmonton, and the University of Bergen, Norway. Whitehouse began exhibiting in 1962 and has participated in such shows as *Manisphere*, Winnipeg, 1970; *Banff Staff Show*, Peter Whyte Gallery, Banff, 1975; and the *Canadian Society of Artists Working in Watercolour*, travelling exhibition, 1977. She was represented in a three-person show at the SUB Gallery, the University of Alberta, Edmonton, which also travelled to Medicine Hat, Alberta, 1979; and her work appeared in a two-person show, *Savage/Whitehouse*, Gallery 111, Winnipeg, Manitoba, 1978. Solo exhibitions were held at Latitude 53 Gallery, Edmonton, 1977, and Arthur Street Gallery, Winnipeg, 1979.

Whitehouse works with watercolour on paper and with acrylic on canvas. The size of her watercolours is 54 cm x 60 cm, while her canvases are generally large, averaging 215 cm x 150 cm. The colours she uses in both media are soft and muted. The acrylic is applied in a combination of thin washes as well as in painterly sections. The negative areas of paper and canvas play a large role in the overall composition.

Diane Whitehouse can be reached c/o Harry Savage, 9820-92 Avenue, Edmonton, Alberta.

Title and date untitled 1976
Medium watercolour, paper
Size 37 cm x 28 cm

Thelma Manarey

Edmonton born Thelma Manarey was educated at the Southern Alberta Institute of Technology, Calgary, as well as through summer courses at the Banff Centre School of Fine Arts and at the University of Washington. She has furthered her education through a variety of workshops, including Emma Lake, Saskatchewan, 1960 and 1963, and courses with the Faculty of Extension, University of Alberta, Edmonton.

Since 1965 Manarey has been the recipient of four major awards, including the Performing and Creative Arts Award, Visual Arts, City of Edmonton, 1973. Her works are found in many private collections in Edmonton and in Alberta House, London, England. Manarey exhibits mainly in Edmonton, although she has participated in group shows across Canada and in Oregon. She has also been commissioned to paint several official government portraits.

Although best known for her miniature etchings, Manarey also paints with acrylic, watercolour, and oils. While she generally uses figurative imagery, her larger abstract canvases feature white pigment on a coloured ground in order to emphasize positive versus negative space. Her desire is "to achieve simplicity with content, whether it is in pencil, oils, watercolour, or acrylic, whether the format is large or small, whether the subject matter is realistic or abstract. My concern is with negative and positive space and in the use of colour. I paint what, and as, I choose."

Manarey can be reached at her studio address of 12026-93 Street, Edmonton, Alberta.

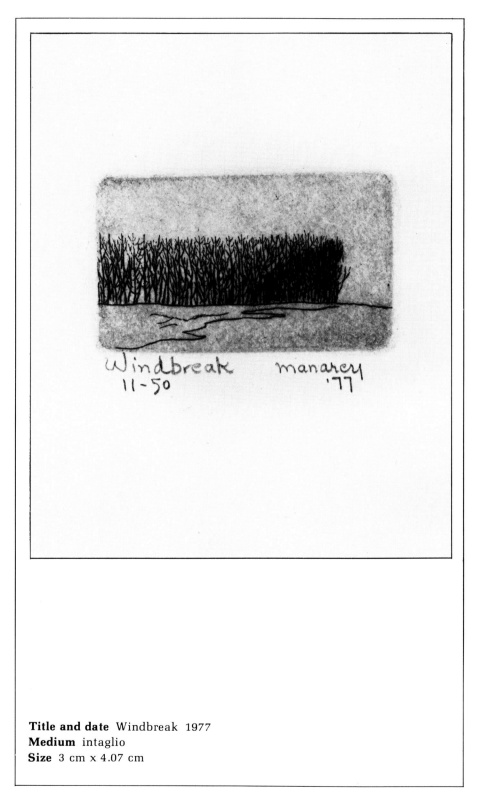

Title and date Windbreak 1977
Medium intaglio
Size 3 cm x 4.07 cm

Jean LaPointe Mihalcheon

Jean LaPointe Mihalcheon was born in Domremy, Saskatchewan, in 1929. She received a diploma from the Alberta College of Art, Calgary, 1953, where she also completed post-graduate studies in glaze technology, 1975. She is a sessional instructor of design with the Adult Education Program, Alberta College of Art, Calgary, and also with the Kerby Centre for Senior Citizens, Calgary.

Mihalcheon received the Henry Birks & Sons Award for General Excellence, 1951, and an Alberta Visual Arts Award, 1952. She is represented in the following permanent collections: the City of Calgary Civic Collection; the Alberta Art Foundation, Edmonton;

Government House, Edmonton; Alberta House, London, England; the Government of Manitoba, Winnipeg, Manitoba; as well as private and corporate collections in Western Canada. Mihalcheon held one-person shows at Calgary Galleries, Calgary, 1974; Fleet Gallery, Winnipeg, Manitoba, 1975; and Mount Royal College, Calgary, 1978. She has participated in group shows at the Alberta College of Art, Calgary, 1974; Chapman Galleries, Red Deer, 1974; Peter Whyte Gallery, Banff, 1975; and was included in *The Fine Art of Alberta Craft*, the XI Commonwealth Games, Edmonton, 1978; and *The Works*, SUB Gallery, University of Alberta, Edmonton, 1979.

Mihalcheon's interests can be divided into two major areas, relief murals and ceramic heads. The murals are based on landscape imagery. She combines slab and wheel-thrown porcelain forms which are fired with oxide glazes and mounted on a painted, plywood backing. The heads, also in porcelain, are decorative sculptural forms approximately thirty-five centimetres high and are not meant to be portraits. They are initially wheel-thrown forms with detail added through hand manipulation and slab constructions.

Mihalcheon often works on commission and can be contacted through her home at 23 Cambridge Road NW, Calgary, Alberta.

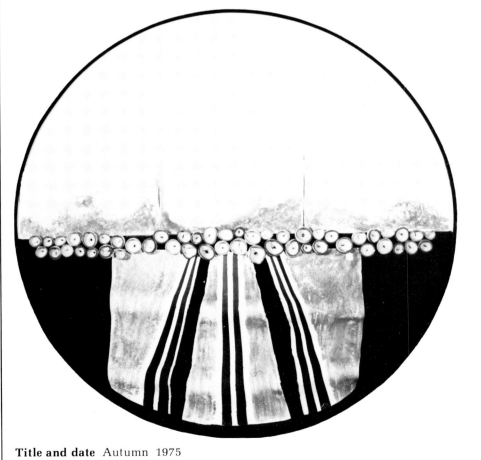

Title and date Autumn 1975
Medium porcelain and plywood
Size 121 cm (diameter)

Janusz Malinowski

Jan Malinowski is a graduate of the University of Alberta, Edmonton, and the Academy of Fine Arts, Warsaw, Poland. In 1970 and 1971 he attended the University of Alberta, Edmonton, as a special student in fine arts. Since that time he has been involved with art education and commercial silk-screening and display work.

His work has been collected by the Alberta Art Foundation, Edmonton, and the City Medical Clinic, Central Warsaw, Poland. For the last eight years Malinowski has participated in an average of one group show per year. He held a one-person show at the Edmonton Public Library Gallery, 1974. All of the shows have taken place in Edmonton, with the exception of a group show at the Galeria Dom Artysty, Warsaw, Poland, in 1975.

Malinowski paints with both acrylic and watercolour and has produced drawings in pen and ink as well as graphite. His surrealistic imagery is achieved through a rich application of acrylic paint applied in thin washes and is often based on still life within a landscape space. Watercolour is applied on smooth paper in small, irregular shapes which are slowly built up until the desired imagery is evoked. The white of the paper is incorporated as a basic element of the composition.

Janusz Malinowski usually spends the summer season working with the Forestry Department, Government of Alberta, in a fire-tower in the northern part of the province. However, he can be reached through the mail at his home at 11, 112A-8 Avenue SE, Calgary, Alberta.

Title and date Still Life 1977
Medium acrylic on linen
Size 63.5 cm x 91 cm

Norman Yates

Norman Yates was born in Calgary in 1923. He was on the executive of the University Art Association of Canada, 1971 to 1973, and the Chairman of the Alberta Art Foundation, Edmonton, 1976-77. He teaches with the Department of Art and Design at the University of Alberta, Edmonton.

Yates received a Canada Council Senior Arts Award in 1967 and 1975 and the City of Edmonton Performing and Creative Arts Award—Visual Arts, 1972. His work may be found in the National Gallery of Canada, Ottawa, Ontario; the Canada Council Art Bank, Ottawa, Ontario; the Alberta Art Foundation, Edmonton; the Faculty Club, University of Alberta, Edmonton; and many civic collections. He has had solo exhibitions in the United States, Great Britain, Germany, and Canada, at such centres as the Glenbow-Alberta Institute, Calgary, 1977; Beaverbrook Art Gallery, Fredericton, New Brunswick, 1978; and the Art Gallery of Nova Scotia, Halifax, Nova Scotia, 1978. Yates has been commissioned to paint several murals, including the exterior of the Engineering Building, the University of Alberta, Edmonton, and an interior work for the Centennial Library, Edmonton. Group exhibitions include *Vision '77*, Phillips Art Gallery, Banff, 1977; *Albertawork*, the University of Calgary and the Alberta College of Art, Calgary, 1977; and *Alberta Landscape*, the Edmonton Art Gallery, Edmonton, 1979.

Norman Yates's large horizontal canvases accentuate the endless horizon of the prairie landscape. "Man is subordinate to the landscape through a feeling of the continuous, infinite extension of the prairie in every direction." Yates terms this portrayal of endless countryside as "landspace." "I have a conviction that the history and the development of the prairies is integral with a love for the land. We discard that love and we lose our soul. My drawings and paintings are based on the landspace and the people I find there."

His studio is located ninety-six kilometres west of Edmonton and provides an uninterrupted view of Alberta's landscape. Yates can be contacted through the Department of Art and Design, the University of Alberta, Edmonton, Alberta.

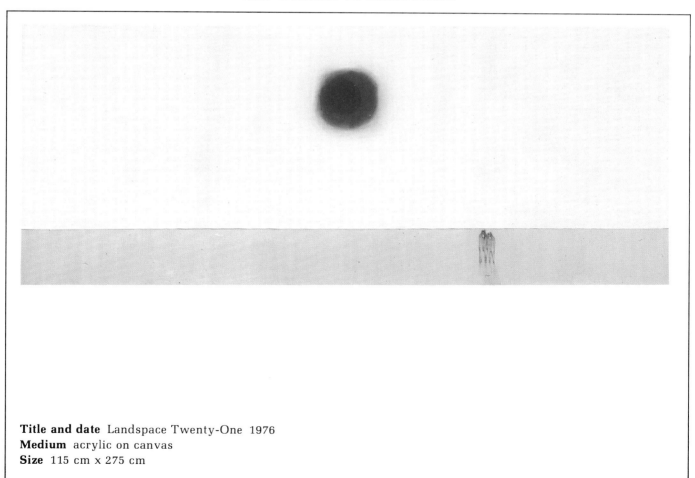

Title and date Landspace Twenty-One 1976
Medium acrylic on canvas
Size 115 cm x 275 cm

Pirkko Karvonen

Pirkko Karvonen was born in Forssa, Finland, in 1935. She began weaving in her homeland as a teenager and moved to Alberta in 1951. In the early 1970s she returned to Finland for a short time to study with a textile designer. Since 1969 Karvonen has been instructing weaving throughout the province and has been instrumental in the founding of the Hand Weavers, Spinners, and Dyers of Alberta and the Strathcona County Weavers.

She has received several awards, including a Government of Alberta grant to attend the World Crafts Council in Ixtepec, Mexico, 1976. She has participated in over twenty group exhibitions since 1971.

Karvonen experiments with a variety of materials. She uses both Finnish and Canadian yarns, including Alberta fleece. Natural dyes prepared by the artist are used to dye the fleece. Nature is the chief source of inspiration for both the colour and the design elements in her work, although some of her pieces are inspired by ancient mythology. Karvonen produces yardage for clothing, practical items such as place mats and rugs, as well as wall-hangings. The hangings can range from small decorator pieces to large architectural commissions reaching 274 centimetres in length.

Her studio is at Box 8, Site 11, R.R.2, Sherwood Park, Alberta.

Title and date Eclipse 1977
Medium handloomed, brown and cream wool
Size 135 cm x 145 cm

Ron Kostyniuk

Ron Kostyniuk was born in 1941 in Saskatchewan. He received a Bachelor of Arts and a Bachelor of Education from the University of Saskatchewan, Saskatoon, Saskatchewan, and a Master of Science and a Master of Fine Arts from the University of Wisconsin, Minnesota. He has been instructing in the Department of Art and Design, University of Calgary, since 1971.

Awards include a University of Alberta undergraduate scholarship, Canada Council grants in 1975, 1976, and 1978, and a University of Wisconsin Graduate Fellowship in 1970. He was elected to the Royal Academy of Fine Arts. Kostyniuk's work may be found in many corporate collections; in the Alberta Art Foundation, Edmonton; the Canada Council Art Bank, Ottawa, Ontario; Mendel Art Gallery, Saskatoon, Saskatchewan; the Ukrainian Institute of Modern art, Chicago, Illinois; the Edmonton Art Gallery, Edmonton; and several university collections across Canada. Kostyniuk exhibits in Canada and the United States. From 1965 to 1979 he has had nineteen one-person shows in centres such as the Glenbow Art Institute, Calgary, 1972; the Beaverbrook Art Gallery, Fredericton, New Brunswick, 1973; the Ukrainian Institute of Modern Art, Chicago, Illinois, 1973; and Mt. St. Vincent University, Halifax, Nova Scotia, 1975. He has also participated in many group shows, including *Prairie Painters*, the Edmonton Art Gallery, Edmonton, 1974; *Our World*, Confederation Centre, Charlottetown, Prince Edward Island, 1972; and the *Seventh Biennal of Canadian Painting*, National Gallery of Canada, Ottawa, Ontario, 1968.

Kostyniuk is primarily concerned with what he terms "the relief idiom" and the evolution of the coloured space-plane in his sculpture. He generally works in painted plexi-glass, although he has experimented in wood. The majority of his sculptures are very large, complex constructions of multiple coloured planes in a geometric composition.

Kostyniuk can be reached through the Department of Art and Design, the University of Calgary, Calgary, or at his home at 4907 Viceroy Drive NW, Calgary, Alberta.

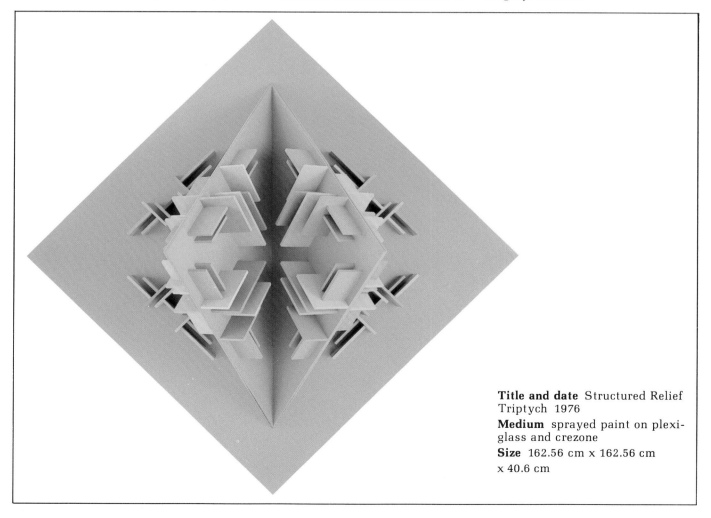

Title and date Structured Relief Triptych 1976
Medium sprayed paint on plexi-glass and crezone
Size 162.56 cm x 162.56 cm x 40.6 cm

Brenda Campbell

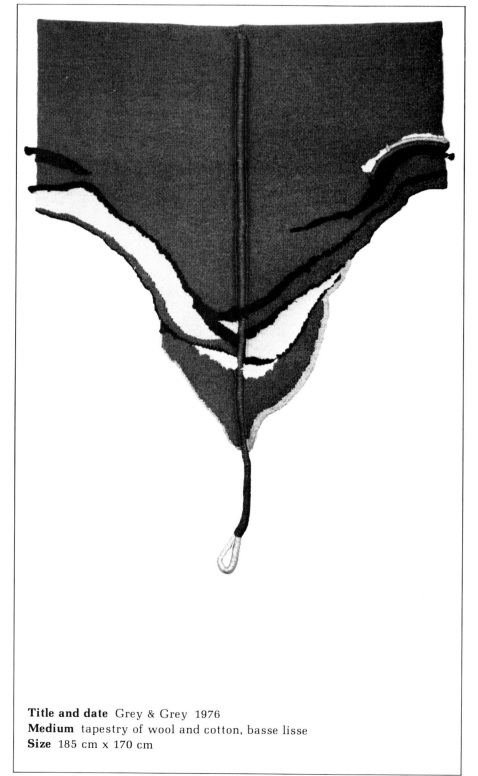

orn in Moose Jaw, Saskatchewan, in 1942, Brenda Campbell attended the Alberta College of Art, Calgary.

Her fibre work received the Award of Excellence in *Faces of Canada*, Montreal, Quebec, 1976. Her weavings can be found in many corporate collections in Calgary and Edmonton, as well as in Alberta House, London, England, and the Alberta Art Foundation, Edmonton. Campbell has participated in several exhibitions since 1969, including *Wool Gatherings '73*, Montreal, Quebec, 1973; *Satori West*, Calgary, 1973; *Alberta Art Foundation Exhibition*, Sapporo, Japan, 1974; *Alberta Art Foundation European Exhibition*, travelling tour, 1975; *Faces of Canada*, Montreal, Quebec, 1976; and *The Fine Art of Alberta Craft*, the XI Commonwealth Games, Edmonton, 1978.

Campbell has maintained a studio in Calgary since 1971. She is a tapestry weaver, and a great deal of her work is commissioned. "Each weaving becomes a part of the last and a part of the next. I always enjoy working on pieces I sometimes refer to as 'my own work,' where I have found greater freedom to be able to experiment and grow."

Brenda Campbell lives at 2333 Osborne Crescent SW, Calgary, Alberta.

Title and date Grey & Grey 1976
Medium tapestry of wool and cotton, basse lisse
Size 185 cm x 170 cm

Neil Fiertel

Sculptor Neil Fiertel was born in New York City in 1941. He completed a Bachelor of Science in bio-psychology at the University of Chicago, a Bachelor of Arts in sculpture at the University of Miami, and a Master of Visual Arts in sculpture at Florida State University. Fiertel became a Canadian citizen in 1975 and is an associate professor at the University of Alberta.

Public collections containing his work are the Alberta Art Foundation, Edmonton, the University of Alabama, and several corporate buildings in Miami, Florida. Fiertel has held four one-person shows since 1973 and has exhibited in such group shows as *Works in Clay*, Latitude 53 Gallery, Edmonton, 1979; *Obsessions Rituals Controls*, Norman Mackenzie Gallery, Regina, Saskatchewan, 1978; and *Sculptors*, Latitude 53 Gallery, Edmonton, 1976.

Fiertel has been sculpting professionally since 1969. In 1973 his work underwent a radical change of direction from abstract and non-figurative form toward highly emotive and decidedly figurative images. The human figure is the motivating force in his work, and he uses human scale to attempt to heighten the relationship between viewer and sculpture. The figures average 100 centimetres in height.

Fiertel may be reached at his studio address Box 5, Site 7, R.R.2, Winterburn, Alberta, or through the Department of Art and Design, the University of Alberta, Edmonton, Alberta.

Title and date Strongman 1977
Medium ceramic, unglazed
Size 100 cm (height)

Bruce O'Neil

Bruce O'Neil was born in Winnipeg, Manitoba, 1942. He studied at the Alberta College of Art, Calgary, 1961 to 1964, and the Instituto Allende, Mexico, 1965. He has acted as a guest, artist, and teacher at several art institutes across Canada.

O'Neil received an Alberta Visual Arts Scholarship, 1963; an Instituto Allende Scholarship, 1964; a Canada Council Materials Grant, 1968; a Canada Council Arts Grant, 1975; and a Canada Council Travel Grant, 1977-78. He is represented in a number of public and private collections, including the Government of Alberta, Edmonton; the Alberta College of Art, Calgary; the Canada Council Art Bank, Ottawa, Ontario; the Edmonton Art Gallery, Edmonton; the Law Courts Building of Edmonton; Memorial University, St. John's, Newfoundland; and corporate collections across Canada.

Since 1966 O'Neil has had several solo exhibitions; the most recent have been at the University of Saskatoon, Saskatchewan, 1977; the Southern Alberta Art Gallery, Lethbridge, 1977; Canadian Art Galleries, Calgary, 1977 and 1978; the Mira Godard Galleries in Toronto, Ontario, 1977; Montreal, Quebec, 1978; and Calgary, 1980. His work has also been shown in a succession of important group shows, some of which are *14 Canadians; a Critic's Choice*, Hirshhorn Museum and Sculpture Garden, Smithsonian Institution, Washington, D.C., 1977; *Painting Now*, Agnes Etherington Centre, Queen's University, Kingston, Ontario, 1977; *Certain Traditions: Recent British and Canadian Art*, Edmonton Art Gallery, Edmonton, 1978; *Vision '78*, Walter Phillips Gallery, Banff, Alberta, 1978; and *Seven Prairie Painters*, the Art Gallery of Ontario, Toronto, Ontario, 1978-79.

In the past O'Neil's abstract acrylic canvases have been noted for their worked and painterly surfaces. Paint was applied in a variety of methods such as pouring, staining, scraping, and brushing. The approach was insistent, and the use of space, the awareness of light, and the imagery alluded to the prairie environment. Works completed in 1978 to 1980 are more lyrical in their loosely stained and vibrant background. O'Neil also produces lithographs and mixed-media works on paper, using pencil, pastels, charcoal, and ink.

His home and studio is at 2006-30 Avenue SW, Calgary, Alberta.

Title and date Twist & Flip 1979
Medium acrylic on canvas
Size 125 cm x 212.5 cm

John Hall

John Hall was born in Edmonton in 1943. He studied at the Alberta College of Art, Calgary, and the San Miguel de Allende, Mexico. Hall teaches painting and drawing at the University of Calgary.

He has been the recipient of several Canada Council Project and Travel Grants and was elected to membership in the Royal Canadian Academy of Arts in 1975. He is represented in the permanent collections of the following art galleries and museums: the National Gallery of Canada, Ottawa, Ontario; the Canada Council Art Bank, Ottawa, Ontario; Glenbow-Alberta Institute, Calgary; Montreal Museum of Fine Arts, Montreal, Quebec; the University of Calgary, Calgary; Confederation Art Gallery and Museum, Charlottetown, Prince Edward Island; Memorial University, Newfoundland;

the Alberta Art Foundation, Edmonton; and the Calgary Civic Collection, Calgary. Recent one-person shows include *John Hall: Paintings & Auxiliary Works*, a nine-year retrospective at the Alberta College of Art Gallery, Calgary, 1978; the National Gallery, Ottawa, Ontario, 1979; University of Alberta, SUB Gallery, Edmonton, 1972; and the Alberta College of Art Gallery, Calgary, 1970. He has exhibited in many group shows, including *Alberta Artists*, Artcore, Vancouver, British Columbia, 1979; *What's New*, Edmonton Art Gallery, Edmonton, 1976; *Albertawork*, the Alberta College of Art Gallery, Calgary, 1977; and *Selected Works from the Alberta Art Foundation*, European travelling tour, 1975-76.

Hall uses an assemblage or maquette of found objects and materials such as

cloth, wire, tires, cardboard, satin, and plastic flowers to construct a model for his imagery. Plastic dolls and silk, pearls and metal screws may be juxtaposed, all nailed or stretched inside a wooden frame and painted larger than life. Hall feels that the composition itself has no specific meaning or content but that "the artist reveals himself, projects himself, not through subject matter or form but through surface. It is the touching, the caressing of the surface [of the canvas] by the artist that results in meaning;...the other aspects of the work are simply conduits." Hall paints with acrylic on canvas, and the scale of his work ranges from 183 cm x 183 cm to very large sectional canvases.

Hall lives at 19 Rosetree Road NW, Calgary, Alberta.

Title and date Grace 1977
Medium acrylic on canvas
Size 183 cm x 183 cm

Michael Mott

Born in London, England, in 1948, Michael Mott attended technical college in London, England, as well as the Northern Alberta Institute of Technology, Edmonton, where he studied sixteen millimetre motion-picture techniques. His art education was received at the Banff Centre School of Fine Arts, through study grants from the University of Alberta, Edmonton, in 1973 and 1976. Mott also received a purchase award for sculpture at the Banff Centre in 1973. At present, he is the self-employed manager of Professional Scale Modelbuilding Company Limited, which builds miniatures of anything and everything.

His art work is in the collections of the Banff Centre, Banff; the Alberta Art Foundation, Edmonton; and the Government of Alberta, Edmonton. Michael Mott has participated in several exhibitions since 1968, including solo shows at Latitude 53 Gallery, Edmonton, 1976, and the Dandelion Gallery, Calgary, 1976. Group exhibitions include a juried show at Stockton State College, Pomona, New Jersey, 1975; a group show at the SUB Gallery, the University of Alberta, Edmonton, 1977; and *The Fine Art of Alberta Craft*, the XI Commonwealth Games, Edmonton, 1978.

Mott's sculptures are usually multimedia constructions of wood, rope, metal, and clay. Craftsmanship is stressed in all pieces, and the work often has a humorous element. The pieces are usually very complex, and the time span between the generation of the idea and its realization can be up to several months. Ideas are formulated on paper and developed further as the materials are accumulated. All of Mott's sculptures invite the viewer to participate and touch the work.

Mott can be reached at 10415-133 Street, Edmonton, Alberta.

Title and date Tubular Bell Piano 1976
Medium wood, stainless steel, brass, ebony
Size 135 cm x 108.5 cm x 76 cm

Whynona Yates

Born in Leicester, England, in 1926, Whynona Yates emigrated to Canada in 1946. She teaches with the Art and Crafts Division, Students' Union Building, the University of Alberta, Edmonton.

Awards include a Canada Council Research Grant in 1967-68, award of excellence, *Wool Gatherings*, Montreal, Quebec, 1973, as well as certificates of appreciation for her contribution to the Canadian Government Pavilion, Expo 67, Montreal, Quebec, 1976. Collections containing Yates's work are the Department of External Affairs, Ottawa, Ontario; the National Gallery of Canada, Ottawa, Ontario; the Faculty Club, the University of Alberta, Edmonton; the Alberta Art Foundation, Edmonton; and several corporate collections in Edmonton. Although the majority of her work is done on commission, Whynona Yates has participated in group shows in Calgary, the United States, Europe, Mexico, and Japan. One-person shows include the Edmonton Art Gallery, Edmonton, 1973, and Strathcona Place, Edmonton, 1974.

Yates always works in wool and usually spins and dyes the materials herself. She often works with qiviut, the soft under-hair of the musk-ox. She is in the process of studying Japanese to further her research into textiles and craftmanship in fibre work of contemporary and historical Japan. Most of her weavings are large in scale and may take three months to one year to complete. Yates has completed commissioned works of up to 155 cm x 305 cm. The winter is her most productive period, leaving the summers free for researching native dyes and ancient textiles as well as for the sorting and washing of fleece.

Her studio is located at 11035-84 Avenue, Edmonton, Alberta.

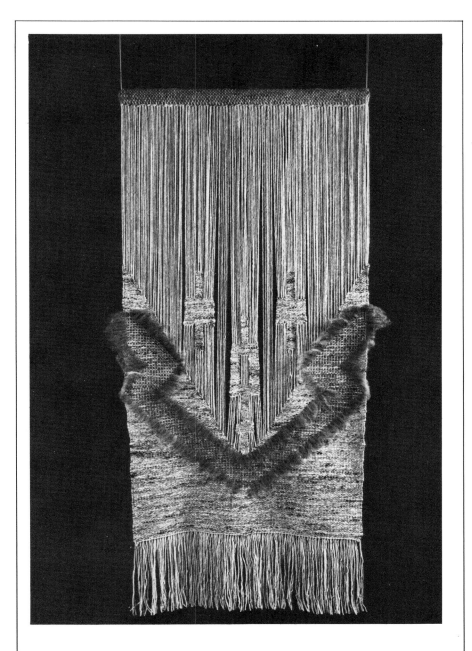

Title and date untitled 1977
Medium wool
Size 145 cm x 63 cm

Alex Janvier

Alex Janvier was born on the Cold Lake Indian Reservation, Alberta, in 1935. He received early recognition of his talent while a student at the Blue Quills Indian Residential School, St. Paul. Janvier continued his studies at the Alberta College of Art, Calgary, from which he graduated in 1960.

His work can be found in numerous large permanent collections and civic collections, some of which are the Canada Council Art Bank, Ottawa, Ontario; the McMichael Canadian Collection, Kleinburg, Ontario; the Museum of Man, Ottawa, Ontario; the Lester B. Pearson Collection, Ottawa, Ontario; the Department of Northern and Indian Affairs, Ottawa, Ontario; and the Saidye and Samuel Bronfman Memorial Collection, Montreal, Quebec. Janvier has been painting professionally since 1971 and has completed many commissioned murals for large public centres such as the Indian Pavilion, Expo 67, Montreal, Quebec; the County of Strathcona Building, Sherwood Park; and the Muttart Conservatory, Edmonton. He has had many one-person shows in major centres across Canada, as well as in Europe, including Stenhusgarden, Linköping, Sweden, 1977, and the Royal Ontario Museum, Toronto, Ontario, 1978.

Janvier's art promotes the culture of his Chipewyan heritage through Janvier utilizing traditional native symbolism in a contemporary non-figurative format to reinforce the qualities of mystique and spirituality of the Déné (people). Recognizable symbols of the Chipewyan Indian such as thunderbirds, arrows, and legendary figures can often be found in his work.

Janvier can be contacted through Janvier Murals and Fine Arts, Box 130, Cold Lake, Alberta.

Title and date Fast Rise 1976
Medium gouache on paper
Size 51 cm x 41 cm

Douglas Motter

Douglas Motter was born in Chicago, Illinois, in 1913. He has been a resident of Calgary since 1919 and received a Bachelor of Fine Arts from the University of Missouri in 1935. He taught at the Alberta College of Art, Calgary, from 1960 to 1977. Motter started weaving as a hobby in 1945 and formed the custom hand-weaving business, Douglas Motter and Associates, in 1961.

Motter received a purchase award in *Craft Dimensions*, Toronto, Ontario, 1969. His watercolours can be found in private collections at the Alberta Art Foundation, Edmonton. His weavings have been commissioned or purchased by many corporate collections, as well as the Legislative Building, Edmonton; the Glencoe Club, Calgary; the Convention Center, Calgary; and the Alberta Art Foundation, Edmonton. Motter has held a number of one-person exhibitions of his weavings and was invited to participate in the Canadian craft fairs held at the World's Fair in Brussels, Belgium, 1958, and Expo 67, Montreal, Quebec, 1967. Other shows include *Craft Dimensions*, Toronto, Ontario, 1969; *Environment*, Edmonton, 1970; and *Environment*, Calgary, 1971. A one-person retrospective of his watercolours was held at Calgary Art Galleries, Calgary, 1973.

Although he sold Douglas Motter and Associates in 1979, he continues to weave. Motter also paints in watercolour, drawing his imagery directly from forms in nature.

Douglas Motter can be reached at 205-33 Avenue SW, Calgary, Alberta.

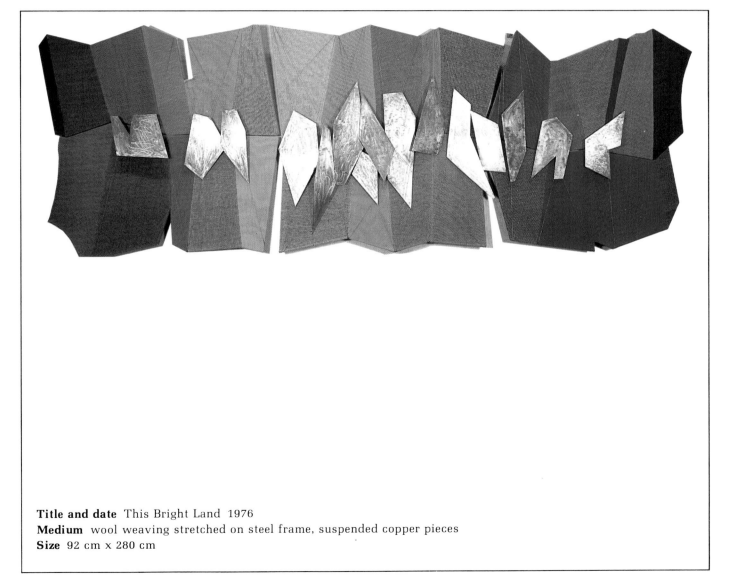

Title and date This Bright Land 1976
Medium wool weaving stretched on steel frame, suspended copper pieces
Size 92 cm x 280 cm

Christina Greco

Christina Greco was born in 1951 in New York City. She received a Bachelor of Arts, with a major in art history, from the University of New York at Buffalo, New York, 1973, and a Master of Fine Arts from the Tyler School of Art, Temple University, Philadelphia, Pennsylvania, 1975, with a major in metal sculpture. Between 1975 and 1979 she instructed at the Alberta College of Art, Calgary.

Christina Greco has work in private collections in Alberta and has participated in exhibitions in Buffalo, New York, 1973; Philadelphia, Pennsylvania, 1975; Wilmington, Delaware, 1974; and *What's New*, the Edmonton Art Gallery, 1977. A two-person show was held at the Marion Locks Gallery, Philadelphia, Pennsylvania.

Greco has been actively producing fabricated and machined metal objects for several years. Her sculptures are constructed of precious and semiprecious metals such as sterling silver, brass, bronze, and aluminum. These metals are often used in combination with other materials, including plastics and fibre. Her sculptures are small, intimate pieces displaying delicate and precise craftsmanship.

Christina Greco lives at 1307-10 Street SW, Calgary, Alberta.

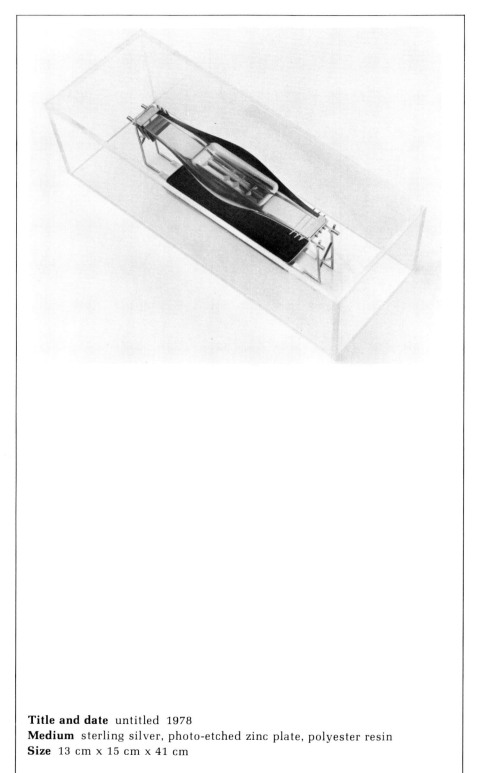

Title and date untitled 1978
Medium sterling silver, photo-etched zinc plate, polyester resin
Size 13 cm x 15 cm x 41 cm

Gary Olson

Born in Minneapolis, Minnesota, in 1946, Gary Olson received a Bachelor of Fine Arts degree from the Minneapolis College of Art and Design, Minneapolis, Minnesota, 1969, and a Master of Fine Arts degree from Indiana University, Bloomington, Indiana, 1973. Olson is currently an instructor of drawing and printmaking at the Alberta College of Art, Calgary.

His work has been purchased for permanent collections in Europe, the United States, and Canada, including the Indiana University Museum, Bloomington, Indiana; the Art Gallery of Brant, Brantford, Ontario; the Medical Art Gallery, Saskatoon, Saskatchewan; the Pavillon d'Exposition, Krakow, Poland; the Canada Council Art Bank, Ottawa, Ontario; and the Al-

berta Art Foundation, Edmonton. His work is also hung in nine United States embassies. Olson has held one-person exhibitions at Normandale College, Bloomington, Indiana, 1971; the Indiana University Museum, Bloomington, Indiana, 1973; Europa Gallery, Melbourne, Australia, 1975; the Edmonton Art Gallery, Edmonton, 1976; and Aggregation Gallery, Toronto, Ontario, 1979. He has also exhibited extensively in international graphics exhibitions, including *Printmaking: An Open Medium*, Minneapolis College of Art and Design, Minneapolis, Minnesota, 1977; *Drawings By 12 Canadian Artists*, Thomas Gallery, Winnipeg, 1978; the *13th International Biennale of Graphic Art '79*, Moderna Galerija, Ljubljana, Yugoslavia, 1979; and *Graphex 7*, Art Gallery of Brant, Brantford, 1979.

Olson takes the concept of the picture plane quite literally in his recent drawings. He creates an illusion of a three-dimensional image existing in a specific space on a flat two-dimensional surface. Self-portraits and animal studies result in a satirical statement on the concept of picture plane as Olson both confirms and denies its existence in his work. His interest in this series developed from attempting to instil in students an awareness of the theoretical existence of the picture plane as an integral part of image making. Olson also works in lithography and intaglio.

Olson can be contacted at his home address of 57 Benchlands Drive, Cochrane, Alberta, or through the Alberta College of Art, 1301-16 Avenue NW, Calgary, Alberta.

Title and date I Am Breaking Up My Form On and Beyond the Picture Plane 1977
Medium graphite on paper
Size 75 cm x 100 cm

Don Kottman

on Kottman was born in 1946 in St. Louis, Missouri. He graduated with a Bachelor of Fine Arts from the University of Kansas in 1968 and a Master of Fine Arts from the University of Washington in 1970. He immigrated to Canada in 1974 and teaches painting and drawing at the Alberta College of Art, Calgary.

Kottman received an honourable mention, *Mid-West Annual,* Kansas City, Missouri, 1968, and a Memorial Scholarship for tuition from the University of Washington, Seattle, Washington, 1969. His work is included in the following collections: the Southern Alberta Institute of Technology, Calgary; the Alberta Art Foundation, Edmonton; Alberta Culture, Edmonton; and several corporate collections in Calgary. Solo exhibitions have been held at Mount Royal College Gallery, Calgary, 1976; the Alberta College of Art, Calgary, 1976; the University of Calgary Gallery, Calgary, 1977; and Moos Gallery, Calgary, 1979. He has participated in group shows such as *Making Marks,* the Norman Mackenzie Art Gallery, Regina, Saskatchewan, 1978; *Albertawork,* the Alberta College of Art and the University of Calgary, Calgary, 1977; and *Summer '79,* Moos Gallery, Toronto, 1979.

Kottman has experimented in the past with a collage approach, using a variety of gathered paper products. He is now working in acrylic on paper. His main concern is with the handling of paint, colour, and surface quality. The paintings are alive and active with bright colours. Vigorous markings score the surface and wind throughout the composition.

Don Kottman works, teaches, and lives in Calgary, Alberta. He can be reached at the Alberta College of Art, 1301-16 Avenue NW, Calgary, Alberta.

Title and date July 1979
Medium acrylic on paper
Size 112 cm x 162 cm

Ron Moppett

Ron Moppett was born in Woking, Surrey, England, in 1945. He studied at the Alberta College of Art, 1963 to 1967, and the Instituto Allende, Mexico, 1968. Moppett has acted as a juror for the Canada Council and has juried various exhibitions within the province.

Moppett was awarded a Canada Council Bursary and Travel Award, 1971-72, and a Canada Council Project Award, 1973, as well as Alberta Visual Arts Board Scholarships in 1964 and 1967. His work is represented in the permanent collections of the National Gallery of Canada, Ottawa, Ontario; the Canada Council Art Bank, Ottawa, Ontario; the Government of Alberta, Edmonton; the Alberta College of Art, Calgary; and the City of Calgary. He has been exhibiting since 1964 and has been represented in many group shows, the most current of which are *Western Untitled*, the Glenbow-Alberta Institute, Calgary, 1976; *Albertawork*, the University of Calgary and the Alberta College of Art, Calgary, 1977; and the *1st Canadian Biennale of Prints and Drawings*, Alberta College of Art Gallery, Calgary, 1978. He mounted a two-person exhibition, *Ron Moppett/John Hall*, University of Lethbridge Gallery, Lethbridge, Alberta, 1976, and held a solo exhibition at the Department of Fine Arts, the University of Calgary, 1979. In 1971 Moppett established the *Rose Museum* which travelled to the Burnaby Art Gallery, Burnaby, British Columbia; the Charlottetown Confederation Centre, Prince Edward Island; the Hamilton Art Gallery, Ontario; and the Glenbow-Alberta Institute, Calgary, in 1973.

Moppett's works are assemblages of a wide variety of materials. These found materials, such as wood, cardboard, cloth, glass, and painted images, are pieced together over a period of time. "Their content is on the surface [choice] and in the narrative of rather disparate visual clues." His work has become more three dimensional over the last few years, with less use of the painted image evident in his work between 1976 and 1977.

Ron Moppett lives at 319-11 Street NW, Calgary, Alberta.

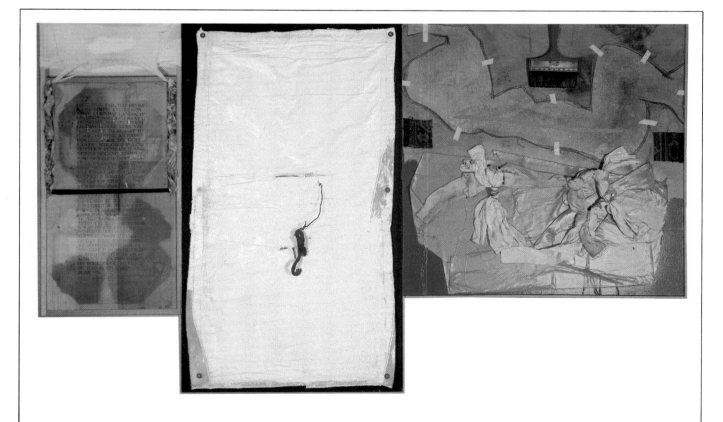

Title and date For Alfred Wallis (No. 2) 1976
Medium mixed media, canvas
Size 136.5 cm x 231 cm

Katie von der Ohe

Born in Peers, Alberta, in 1937, sculptor Katie von der Ohe was educated at the Alberta College of Art, Calgary; the Montreal School of Art and Design, Montreal, Quebec; and the Sculpture Centre, New York. She instructed for many years at the Calgary Allied Arts Centre and has taught at the University of Calgary, the Alberta College of Art, and Mount Royal College, Calgary.

Von der Ohe has received many awards for her work, including a National Gallery Scholarship, 1958; awards from the Sculpture Centre, New York, for study in 1961 and 1963; as well as Canada Council grants in 1963, 1968, 1973, and 1974. Her work has been acquired by the Canada Council Art Bank, Ottawa; the Alberta Art Foundation, Edmonton; the University of Calgary, Calgary; Alberta House,

London, England; and the Sculpture Centre, New York, New York; as well as by private and corporate collections. Solo exhibitions include the Alberta College of Art Gallery, Calgary, 1959, 1964, and 1976; the University of Saskatoon, Saskatoon, Saskatchewan, 1961; 1640 Gallery, Montreal, Quebec, 1966; the University of Alberta, Edmonton, 1972; and the University of Calgary, 1971-72. She has also participated in many group exhibitions and has completed major commissions for the Chinook Mall, Calgary; the Engineering Building, the University of Calgary; the Calgary School Board; several churches in Calgary; and Edmonton Centre, Edmonton.

Figurative and landscape imagery are the important sources of von der Ohe's sculptural concepts. From two-dimensional sketches her ideas are devel-

oped further into three-dimensional models or maquettes through the use of such materials as cardboard, clay, wax, and plaster. Von der Ohe's finished works are realized in a variety of materials, including wood, plastics, plaster, bronze, concrete, and welded, chromed steel. The movable components in her work constantly change the relationship of space and form, and together with the use of highly polished metals they create a sense of weightlessness and invite viewer participation.

Von der Ohe can be reached through the mail at Box 10, Site 27, R.R. 2, Calgary, Alberta.

Title Venetian Puddle
Medium welded steel, chromed and machined
Size 103 cm x 103 cm x 17.5 cm

Garry Jones

G arry Jones was born in Edmonton in 1949 and graduated with a Bachelor of Fine Arts from the University of Alberta in 1972.

He was awarded third prize in the international competition for the Katyn War Memorial, Toronto, Ontario, 1979, and permanent collections containing his work are the University of Alberta, Edmonton; Alberta House, London, England; Government House, Edmonton; and the Alberta Art Foundation, Edmonton. Jones has held solo exhibitions at the SUB Gallery, the University of Alberta, Edmonton, 1975. He was also represented in *Young Contemporaries '76*, organized by the London Art Gallery, London, Ontario, 1976.

Although Garry Jones is primarily interested in sculpting, he also paints. In both expressions he enjoys experimenting with different materials and production procedures. He integrates industrial processes into the development of his work, as he feels that technology is a primary expression of our culture. Air currents and gravity initiate movement in his kinetic pieces. The polished metal surfaces continually reflect a changing environment as the form alters in space. His stable pieces are usually more organic in form, and they range in size from small intimate pieces to large architectural works. He feels that his work is most successful on a commission basis.

Jones can be located at 10709-72 Avenue or at his studio address of 7214-111 Street, Edmonton, Alberta.

Title and date Serpentis 1977
Medium 11 gauge stainless steel sheet, stainless steel cable, 30 lb. counterweight
Size 3.6 m (height)

John Roberts

A graduate from the Cranbrook Academy of Art, Bloomfield Hills, Michigan, in 1965, with a Master of Fine Arts in printmaking, John Roberts also studied at California State University, Northbridge, California, where he received a Bachelor of Fine Arts in graphics and photography in 1970. He was employed as a printer by Gemini GEL, Los Angeles, California, between 1973 and 1975 and by Cirrus Editions Limited, Los Angeles, California, in 1975. He is now a technical demonstrator with the Department of Art and Design, the University of Alberta, Edmonton. John Roberts is on the Visual Arts Committee for Latitude 53 Gallery, Edmonton, and was involved with the print portfolio of ten Commonwealth artists sponsored by the University of Alberta and the XI Commonwealth Games, 1978.

Roberts's work is included in private collections across Europe, the United States, and Canada, as well as in the permanent collections of the Canada Permanent Print Collection, Toronto, Ontario, and the USIA, Brussels, Belgium. His exhibitions include *Alberta-work,* the University of Calgary and the Alberta College of Art, Calgary, 1977; *Robert Gallie Crockett and Drum,* SUB Gallery, the University of Alberta, Edmonton, 1977; *Off the Rack,* Latitude 53 Gallery, Edmonton, 1979; *Images/Aluminum,* Macalaster Galleries, St. Paul, Minnesota, 1979; and *Five from Edmonton,* touring exhibition, Ring House Gallery, Edmonton, 1980.

Roberts has been experimenting with different printmaking processes for several years. His involvement with lithography led to the production of drawings on aluminum plates, using touche washes and coloured dyes. His more recent works are a combination of traditional stone lithography and pastel crayon. He also works with silk-screens.

John Roberts can be reached through the University of Alberta, Edmonton, Alberta, or at his home and studio, 12045-25 Avenue, Edmonton, Alberta.

Title and date untitled 1979
Medium screen print, pastel
Size 35 cm x 56.25 cm

38

Dirk van Wijk

irk van Wijk was born in The Hague, Netherlands, in 1944. He received a Bachelor of Arts from the University of Calgary, 1967; a Master of Arts from the University of Calgary, 1970; and a scholarship for one year of study in art at the Rietveld Academy, Amsterdam, 1967-68. He is a sessional instructor in drawing at the University of Calgary.

Van Wijk has been a member of the Alberta Art Foundation Review Committee for the Calgary area since 1974. His work is represented in the collections of the Glenbow-Alberta Insti-tute, Calgary, and Government House, Edmonton. Van Wijk has held one-man exhibitions at the Calgary Allied Arts Centre, Calgary, 1969; the Dandelion Gallery, Calgary, 1976; and the Mount Royal College Gallery, Calgary, 1977. Since 1969 he has also participated in three two-person exhibitions and several group exhibitions, including *Young Contemporary Calgary Artists' Exhibition*, Alberta College of Art Gallery, Calgary, 1974; *Abstract Works on Paper*, the Edmonton Art Gallery, Edmonton, 1975; *12 Artists from Alberta Work on Paper*, the Alberta College of Art, Calgary, 1976;

and *Canadian Drawings*, the Art Gallery of New Brunswick, Fredericton, New Brunswick, 1976.

Dirk van Wijk completes approximately thirty mixed-media drawings each year. He often works on gesso treated paper, combining silver-point, graphite, coloured pencil, watercolour, and collage techniques. The source of van Wijk's imagery is his "perceptual experience with particular situations such as landscape and still life."

Van Wijk's home is at 81, 7205-4 Street NE, Calgary, Alberta.

Title and date Clouds 1977
Medium mixed media
Size 56 cm x 75 cm

Margaret May

Margaret May was born in Galahad, Alberta, in 1951. She received a Bachelor of Fine Arts degree in 1973 and a Master of Visual Arts degree, printmaking, in 1975 from the University of Alberta, Edmonton. She also studied with Robert Evermon at the Banff Centre School of Fine Arts summer session, Senior Lithography Workshop, in 1977. May is a sessional instructor in printmaking, drawing, and design at the Alberta College of Art in Calgary.

May was awarded a Banff Centre Scholarship, 1977, and a purchase award, *Graphex 5* and *Graphex 7*, Art Gallery of Brant, Brantford, Ontario, 1977 and 1979. Her work can be found in the permanent collections of the Alberta Art Foundation, Edmonton; the Alberta College of Art, Calgary; the University of Alberta Permanent Collection, Edmonton; and the Art Gallery of Brant Collection, Brantford, Ontario. She has been represented in several major group exhibitions since 1972, the most recent of which are the *Survey of Canadian Art Now*, Vancouver Art Gallery, Vancouver, 1974; *Manisphere 11th International Jury Art Show*, Winnipeg, 1974; *The Midwestern*, Winnipeg Art Gallery, Winnipeg, 1976; *Imprint '76*, Graphic Arts Council of Canada, travelling show, Art Gallery of Ontario, Toronto, 1976; *Graphex 7*, the Art Gallery of Brant, Brantford, Ontario, 1979; and *Fifteen*, the Walter Phillips Gallery, Banff, Alberta, 1979.

Although Margaret May has experience with mixed-media processes of printmaking, including photo-lithography, photo-engraving, collography, and relief printing, she is currently involved with the combination of silkscreen, lithography, and relief printing methods.

May can be reached through the Alberta College of Art, 1301-16 Avenue NW, Calgary, Alberta, or at 1104-6 Avenue SW, Calgary, Alberta.

Title and date Three-Cornered Space 1979
Medium lithograph
Size 57 cm x 57 cm

Bonnie Sheckter

Bonnie Sheckter was born in Edmonton in 1951. She graduated from the University of Alberta with a Master of Visual Arts in printmaking in 1976 and taught printmaking at the University of Calgary until the spring of 1977. She is currently a sessional instructor with the Department of Art and Design at the University of Alberta, Edmonton.

Sheckter's various awards include the Coopers & Lybrand Purchase Award, *Imprint '76*; a travel grant, Alberta Culture, for study in the People's Republic of China, Hong Kong, and Japan, 1978; and both a purchase award and a special merit award, *Graphex 7*, Brantford, Ontario, 1979. Her prints may be found in several collections, including the Art Gallery of Brant, Brantford, Ontario; the Alberta Art Foundation, Edmonton; the Print and Drawing Council of Canada; and the National Museum, Poznan, Poland. She has exhibited in international and national exhibitions, including *Intergraphia '78*, Katowice, Poland, 1978; *7th International Print Biennale*, Kracow, Poland, 1978; and *Graphex 7*, the Art Gallery of Brant, Brantford, Ontario, 1979. Recent three-person exhibitions were held at the Hong Kong Arts Centre, Hong Kong, 1978, and the Edmonton Art Gallery, Edmonton, 1979.

Sheckter works with the combination of silk-screen, photo-lithography, and relief printing techniques. Her interest lies in the portrayal of energy, space, movement, and time as visual images, which she captures initially with a camera used as a drawing tool.

Bonnie Sheckter can be reached through the Department of Art and Design, the University of Alberta, Edmonton, Alberta.

Title and date Neon Fugue 1976
Medium photo-lithograph
Size 56 cm x 73.5 cm

Victor Clapp

Victor Clapp was born in Cranbrook, British Columbia, in 1942. He studied at the Alberta College of Art, Calgary, and graduated with a Diploma in Commercial Art in 1966. He has been a resident of Alberta for ten years and his work is included in the Alberta Art Foundation, Edmonton. For nine years Clapp was an exhibit designer with the Provincial Museum and Archives, Edmonton.

He began exhibiting his paintings with the show titled *Alberta '73*, organized by the Edmonton Art Gallery and the Alberta Society of Artists in 1973. His work was among those chosen by the Edmonton Art Gallery for the show *Prairie '74*, as well as those included in the Art Gallery of Hamilton, Hamilton, Ontario, exhibition *9 Out of 10, A Survey of Canadian Art*, 1974.

Clapp works in acrylic on panel board. His paintings are generally small in scale and measure 10 cm x 13 cm to a maximum of 40 cm x 50 cm. A superrealist, his subject matter includes buildings, old vehicles, landscapes, and magnified views of found articles and mechanical objects. Clapp uses a camera extensively to record details, and he usually works from prints and slides.

Clapp works out of his apartment at 1007, 10130-117 Street, Edmonton, Alberta.

Title and date Camper's Legacy 1977
Medium acrylic on masonite
Size 25 cm x 32.5 cm

Bryan Nemish

Bryan Nemish was born in Winnipeg in 1944. He received a Bachelor of Fine Arts degree from the Winnipeg School of Art in 1967. In 1968 he was awarded a Master of Fine Arts degree from the Instituto Allende, San Miguel de Allende, Mexico. He has taught at the Alberta College of Art, Calgary, and the University of Alberta, Edmonton.

Nemish was awarded Canada Council grants in both 1967 and 1968. Other awards include a Graduate Tuition Scholarship from the Instituto Allende, 1967 and 1968. His work has been purchased by the University of Calgary and the Canada Council Art Bank, Ottawa, Ontario, as well as by private collectors across Canada. Solo shows include the Villa de Roma Gallery, San Miguel de Allende, Mexico, 1968; the Alberta College of Art Gallery, Calgary, 1972; and the Edmonton Art Gallery, Edmonton, 1977. He has been represented in various exhibitions in Calgary, Edmonton, and Seattle, Washington, including *14 From Calgary*, Latitude 53 Gallery, Edmonton, 1974; *New Abstract Art*, Edmonton Art Gallery, Edmonton, 1977; and *12 Edmonton Painters*, the Edmonton Art Gallery, Edmonton, 1977.

Nemish paints with acrylic on canvas, and his main concern is with the manipulation of colour and composition as well as with the interrelationship of shape and form within a purely abstract format. "I make statements through paint, through the painted image. It becomes an intricate personal probe, searching for the means to clarify an idea, a stimulus, a felt knowledge. Basically, I am enjoying manipulating and relating to shapes, colours, contrasts, compositions, and forms in purely abstract relationships." His paintings consist of soft and subtle colours moving and intermingling across the surface of the canvas.

Nemish can be located at his studio at 10211-117 Street, Edmonton, Alberta.

Title and date Still 1977
Medium acrylic on canvas
Size 168.5 cm x 96 cm

Illingworth Kerr

Born in Lumsden, Saskatchewan, in 1905, Illingworth Kerr studied at the Ontario College of Art, Toronto, Ontario, between 1924 and 1927. He attended the New Westminster School of Art, London, England, in 1936, and he studied with Hans Hofmann in Massachusetts in 1954. Kerr taught at the Vancouver School of Art, Vancouver, British Columbia, in 1945-46 and was the head of the Alberta College of Art, Calgary, from 1947 to 1967.

Kerr was awarded an honorary doctorate from the University of Calgary, Calgary, 1973; the National Award for Painting and Related Arts, the University of Alberta, Edmonton, 1975; and a Canada Council Fellowship in 1959. He is a member of the Royal Canadian Academy of Arts. Collections containing his paintings include the National Gallery of Canada, Ottawa, Ontario; the Saskatoon Art Gallery, Saskatoon, Saskatchewan; the Alberta Art Foundation, Edmonton; the Glenbow-Alberta Institute, Calgary; Memorial University, St. John's, Newfoundland; the University of Calgary, Calgary; the Norman Mackenzie Gallery, Regina, Saskatchewan; and several corporate and private collections across Canada. Kerr has been painting in Alberta for fifty years. Since his retirement from teaching in 1967, he has produced more work than in his first forty years of painting. He held retrospective exhibitions in 1940, 1962, and 1974, and he has exhibited in more than a dozen one-person shows in the Western and the Maritime provinces since 1967. He is a past member of the Canadian Authors Association and has written several short stories and has illustrated nine publications.

Excluding portrait commissions, Kerr's chief interest has been landscape, especially the prairies and the foothills. He aims at a simple, direct statement of character, mood, and colour. His smaller oils are usually painted on location and are often the sources for his larger canvases, mostly in acrylic, of up to 137 cm x 183 cm. During the past few years, Kerr has spent the winter months painting in Arizona.

Kerr's studio is at 1729-10 Street SW, Calgary, Alberta.

Title and date The Qu'Appelle at Spring Creek Valley 1976
Medium oil on canvas
Size 60 cm x 85.5 cm

Marion Nicoll

Marion Nicoll was born in Calgary and studied at the Ontario College of Art, Toronto, Ontario; the Provincial Institute of Technology and Art, Calgary; and the LCC School of Arts and Crafts, London, England. She also studied under Will Barnet at the Emma Lake Workshop, Emma Lake, Saskatchewan. Marion Nicoll taught design and crafts at the Provincial Institute of Technology and Art, now the Alberta College of Art, Calgary, until 1966. She is a member of the Royal Canadian Academy, the Alberta Society of Artists, and the Print and Drawing Council of Canada.

She was awarded a Canada Council grant in 1958 to study with Barnet and for study and travel in Europe. In 1966 Nicoll received a Canada Council Fellowship. In addition to representation in private collections in Canada and the United states, her work may be found in the collections of the Alberta Art Foundation, Edmonton; the Edmonton Art Gallery, Edmonton; the Glenbow-Alberta Institute, Calgary; the Law Courts Building, Edmonton; the Convention Center, Calgary; the Calgary Public Library, Calgary; and corporate collections in Alberta. She has exhibited widely throughout Canada. Major one-person exhibitions were held at the Edmonton Art Gallery, Edmonton, 1975; the Glenbow-Alberta Institute, Calgary, 1975; in a *Retrospective Print Show* in Edmonton in 1973; and in a touring exhibition on the Western Canada Art Circuit from 1965 to 1966. She was also represented in the *Alberta Art Foundation European Exhibition,* 1975; *Graphex 5,* the Art Gallery of Brant, Brantford, Ontario, 1977; and *Albertawork,* the University of Calgary and the Alberta College of Art, Calgary, 1977. A recent retrospective was held at Masters Gallery, Calgary, 1978.

Her paintings and her prints are distinctive in their bold composition and imagery. Nicoll experiments with many printmaking techniques, including wood-block and clay prints.

Nicoll lives at 7007 Bow Crescent NW, Calgary, Alberta.

Title and date Runes B 1972
Medium cardboard print on paper
Size 40 cm x 38 cm

James McLaren Nicoll

Born in Fort McLeod, Alberta, in 1892, James Nicoll received a Bachelor of Arts in 1922 and a Bachelor of Science in 1924 from the University of Alberta, Edmonton. In 1935 he was elected to the Alberta Society of Artists and was the founding editor of *Highlights*, the Alberta Society of Artists' magazine. He was elected to the presidency of the Society in 1942. Nicoll has been active in the artistic community of Alberta for many years. In 1925 he became a member of the Senate of the University of Alberta, Edmonton, and in 1952 he was elected Chairman of the Visual Arts Committee for the Allied Arts Centre, Calgary.

Permanent collections housing Nicoll's work are the University of Calgary, Calgary; the University of Alberta, Edmonton; the Calgary Allied Arts Council, Calgary; the Canada Council Art Bank, Ottawa, Ontario; the Alberta Art Foundation, Edmonton; the Glenbow-Alberta Institute, Calgary; and Memorial University, St. John's, Newfoundland. One-person exhibitions have been held at the Peter Whyte Gallery, Banff, and the Glenbow Institute, Calgary. Nicoll was also represented in the *Royal Canadian Academy of Arts Jury Exhibition,* 1938, and participated in the *Canadian Society of Painters in Watercolor* exhibitions throughout the 1940s, 1950s, and 1960s. Two-person exhibitions with Marion Nicoll were held at the University of Calgary, Calgary, 1972, and the Glenbow-Alberta Institute, Calgary, 1972.

James Nicoll can be reached at his home at 7007 Bow Crescent NW, Calgary, Alberta.

Title and date Steam 1973
Medium oil on canvas
Size 76.8 cm x 102.2 cm

Graham Peacock

Born in London, England, in 1945, Graham Peacock attended London University Goldsmith's School of Art between 1962 and 1966 and the Leeds College of Art, Yorkshire, England, from 1966 to 1967.

In 1968 he was awarded an Italian government scholarship in painting to study at the British School of Rome. Other awards include the Greater London Council Major Award, 1962 to 1966, and the Hill Trust Fund Purchase Award, 1973. Peacock's work may be found in many permanent collections, some of which are the British Embassy, Rome, Italy; the Canada Council Art Bank, Ottawa, Ontario; Newport Art Gallery, Wales; the Edmonton Court House, Edmonton; and the Edmonton Art Gallery, Edmonton. He has exhibited widely throughout Europe and Canada since 1967. Solo exhibitions have been held at such centres as the Edmonton Art Gallery, Edmonton, 1977; Mount Allison University, Sackville, New Brunswick, 1979; and Glenmore Gallery, Toronto, Ontario, 1979. He has participated in group shows such as *New Abstract Art*, the Edmonton Art Gallery, Edmonton, 1977; *Abstraction West— Emma Lake and After*, the Edmonton Art Gallery, Edmonton, 1976; *Alberta Collects Alberta*, Beaver House Gallery, Edmonton, 1979.

Graham Peacock has painted and sculpted for the majority of his career, although he concentrated on painting between 1969 and 1976. His works are abstract, and his acrylic paintings can range in size from large, mural-scale works on canvas to smaller works on paper. The size of his sculptures ranges from human scale, at the largest, to small table pieces. The surfaces of his painted wood sculptures bear a close relationship to Peacock's work on canvas.

Peacock's studio is at 10048-101A Avenue, 2nd Floor, Edmonton, Alberta.

Title and date Erry Che 1977
Medium acrylic on canvas
Size 166 cm x 85 cm

Walter Jule

Walter Jule was born in Seattle, Washington, in 1940 and graduated from the University of Washington, Seattle, Washington, with a Bachelor of Arts in interior design and a Master of Fine Arts in printmaking and drawing. Post-graduate studies were completed at the University of Arizona, Extension School in Florence, Italy. He has taught at the University of Washington, Seattle, Washington; Montana State University, Bozeman, Montana; and Douglas College, Vancouver, British Columbia. He is now an associate professor and co-ordinator of the Printmaking Division, Department of Art and Design, University of Alberta, Edmonton, where he has been fundamental in the development of printmaking facilities for the past six years.

Jule's work was chosen for inclusion in the *Commonwealth Print Portfolio* to commemorate the XI Commonwealth Games, Edmonton, 1978. This portfolio is in the collection of the National Galleries of Commonwealth countries. His work has been purchased for numerous major collections across Canada, the United States, Poland, and Czechoslovakia. His impressive history of exhibitions includes major centres in Canada, the United States, and Europe. Competitive exhibitions include *Intergraphia '78*, Krakow, Poland, 1978, and *Graphex 7*, the Art Gallery of Brant, Brantford, Ontario, 1979. He was also represented in *Five Canadian Printmakers*, Mitake Gallery, Tokyo, Japan, 1978; *9 Alberta Artists*, Canadian Embassy Gallery, Boston, Massachusetts, 1978;

and the *Eleventh International Biennale Exhibition of Prints in Tokyo*, Japan, 1979.

He uses a variety of techniques, including photo-lithography, photo-silk-screen, and embossing. The quality of the surface is of utmost importance to the artist, and the combination of printmaking techniques gives his finished work the illusion of being suspended between the second and third dimensions.

Walter Jule can be reached through the mail at the Department of Art and Design, University of Alberta, Edmonton, Alberta.

Title and date Suspicions Turned Around 1977
Medium embossed photo-lithograph, photo-silk-screen
Size 56.5 cm x 70.75 cm

Barbara Ballachey

Barbara Ballachey was born in Edmonton in 1949. She studied at McGill University, Montreal, Quebec, the Ecole des Beaux Arts, Montreal, Quebec, and graduated from the University of Alberta with a Bachelor of Fine Arts in 1971.

Her work is displayed in the Alberta Art Foundation, Edmonton; the Canada Council Art Bank, Ottawa, Ontario; the Edmonton Art Gallery, Edmonton; and the Leighton Art Centre, Priddis, Alberta. Solo shows include the Edmonton Art Gallery, Edmonton,

1974; the Dandelion Gallery, Calgary, 1975; and Galerie Royale, Calgary, 1976. She has also participated in many group shows, the most recent of which are the *Winnipeg 14th International Jury Art Show*, Winnipeg, Manitoba, 1977; *New Abstract Art*, the Edmonton Art Gallery, Edmonton, 1977; *Thompson/Ballachey*, Canadian Art Galleries, Calgary, 1977; *The Indomitable Line: Contemporary Canadian Drawings*, the Norman Mackenzie Art Gallery, Regina, Saskatchewan, 1977; and *Selections*, Canadian Art Galleries, Calgary, 1979.

Barbara Ballachey paints with acrylic on canvas as well as with oil on both canvas and paper. Her works on paper are often combinations of watercolour, charcoal, ink, and various other media. Ballachey uses a variety of tools in her painting and drawing process, including rollers, brushes, sponges, and squeegees. All work explores the two-dimensional surface with emphasis on colour and tone.

Ballachey can be contacted through her home address at 8, 908 Memorial Drive NW, Calgary, Alberta.

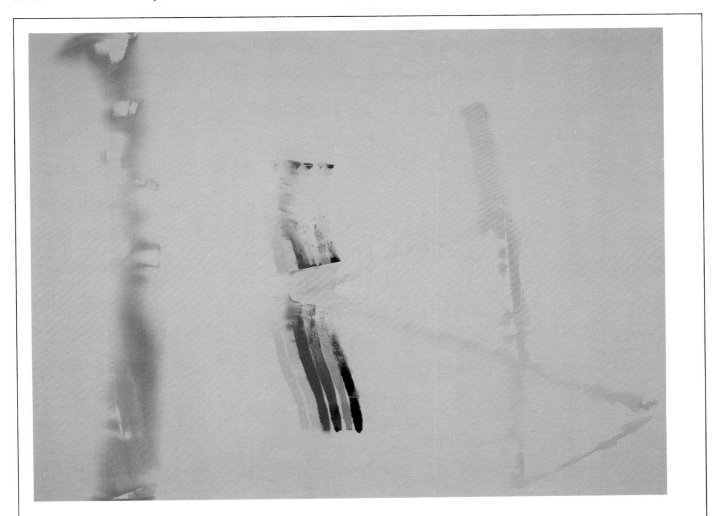

Title and date Swan Series #2 1977
Medium acrylic on canvas
Size 121.5 cm x 162.5 cm

Janet Mitchell

Well-known Calgary artist Janet Mitchell has been exhibiting since 1947. Her many awards include First in Watercolour, *Winnipeg Watercolor Show*, 1960; honourable mention, *All Alberta Show*, 1963; purchase award with medal, *Canadian Society of Painters in Watercolor*, Toronto, Ontario, 1964; and the Sutton and Bell Purchase Award, *Canadian Society of Painters in Watercolor*, Toronto, Ontario, 1974. Her paintings are included in the permanent collections of the National Gallery of Canada, Ottawa, Ontario; Calgary Allied Arts Centre, Calgary; Sarnia Art Gallery, Sarnia, Ontario; Windsor Art Gallery, Windsor, Ontario; the Regina Public Library, Regina, Saskatchewan; the London Public Library and Museum, London, Ontario; and St. John's Memorial Gallery, Newfoundland.

She has been an active member of Alberta's art community for many years and is a member of the Canadian Society of Painters in Watercolour, as well as the Alberta Society of Artists. She was elected to the Royal Canadian Academy in 1977. Mitchell has served in an advisory capacity on the purchasing committee of the Alberta Art Foundation, Edmonton, and is a member of the Calgary Region Art Foundation. Mitchell was commissioned by Readers Digest of Canada and the Montreal Club to paint the John F. Kennedy Rose for the *Rose Festival* at Expo 67, Montreal, Quebec, 1967. She has held one-person shows in major centres across Canada, including Artlenders, Montreal, Quebec, 1969; Fleet Gallery, Winnipeg, Manitoba, 1970; Kensington Gallery, Calgary, 1972; and Calgary Galleries, Calgary, 1973. In 1977 a *Retrospective and New Works* exhibition was shown at the Glenbow Centre, Calgary. Mitchell was also represented in the *Alberta Art Foundation Touring Show* to London, Paris, and Brussels, 1975.

Mitchell paints in both oils and acrylic and has completed many pen-and-ink sketches of the countryside around Calgary. Her work is colourful and spontaneous, often combining human and animal figures floating in a field of bright, intermingling colours. Her work is noted for its combination of humour, fantasy, and colour.

She lives at 85 Capri Avenue NW, Calgary, Alberta.

Title and date Cattle and Birds 1977
Medium watercolour
Size 56 cm x 76 cm

Derek Michael Besant

A graduate from the University of Calgary, Derek Michael Besant was born in Fort MacLeod, Alberta, in 1950. Now on staff at the Alberta College of Art, Calgary, he has been a guest artist at the University Arts Association of Canada Conference, the University of Alberta, Edmonton, and St. Michael's Printshop, Memorial University, St. John's, Newfoundland.

Awards include Canada Council grants in 1975 and 1976 and a Government of Alberta Study and Research Grant in 1973. Permanent collections containing his work are the Art Gallery of Brant, Brantford, Ontario; the Canada Council Art Bank, Ottawa; De Cordova Museum, Massachusetts; the Alberta Art Foundation, Edmonton, as well as corporate and university collections across Canada. Besant has exhibited widely in Canada and has participated in many international exhibitions, including *Timbres et Tampons D'Artistes*, Museum of Art and History, Geneva, Switzerland, 1978; *Sixth British International Biennale*, Bradford Art Galleries and Museum, West Yorkshire, England, 1979; *Thirty-first National Exhibition*, the Boston Printmakers, Brockton Art Center, Massachusetts, 1979; and the *8th International Triennial of Original Coloured Graphic Prints*, the Grenchen Art Society, Haldenschulhaus, Switzerland, 1979.

Besant works on paper in a variety of media, including watercolour, ink, pencil, lithography, and etching. Subject matter is based on everyday household objects depicted in an unusual and unexpected manner to illustrate inert objects in a startling second of movement. Plates shatter in mid-air and bits of cloth float in space. These hypothetical activities always take place within the confines of a room, and the sense of light and the subtly controlled colour give the paintings an ethereal and mystical quality.

He can be contacted through the Alberta College of Art, 1301-16 Avenue NW, Calgary, Alberta, or through the mail at Box 520, Midnapore, Alberta.

Title and date Impartial Observer 1979
Medium watercolour and ink on BFK Rives paper
Size 75 cm x 90 cm

Barbara Roe Hicklin

Born in Toronto, Ontario, Barbara Roe Hicklin studied at the Central Technical School, Toronto, Ontario, and the New York Phoenix School of Design, New York City.

She received a purchase award in the *Canadian Society of Painters in Watercolor* exhibition, 1976, and her paintings may be found in the collections of the Alberta Art Foundation, Edmonton; the Convention Center, Calgary; Alberta Environmental Conservation Authority; Government House, Edmonton; and corporations throughout the province. Hicklin exhibits widely

and has held one-person shows at the Centennial Library Art Gallery, Edmonton, 1970; Canadian Art Galleries, Calgary, 1971 and 1977; Canadian Galleries, Edmonton, 1973; the University of Calgary, Calgary, 1976; and the Nickle Arts Museum, Calgary, 1979. Group shows include *Alberta '73*, the Edmonton Art Gallery, Edmonton, 1973; *Prairie '74*, the Edmonton Art Gallery, Edmonton, 1974; *Alberta Realists*, the Edmonton Art Gallery, Edmonton, 1974; and the *Canadian Society of Painters in Watercolor*, the Glenbow-Alberta Institute, Calgary, 1976.

Hicklin captures in her paintings the effects of light, colour, and space in nature. The technique of adjoining patches of colour produces a visual movement and a sense of depth. The shapes of these individual colour patches emphasize form and distance, blending together as though viewing the landscape imagery through a prism. Her large paintings are watercolour and paper mounted on masonite. Smaller watercolour sketches are completed on location.

Barbara Roe Hicklin lives at 2429 Cherokee Drive NW, Calgary, Alberta.

Title and date Sunny Interval 1977
Medium watercolour on board
Size 106.5 cm x 140 cm

John K. Esler

Born in Manitoba in 1933, John Esler received a Bachelor of Fine Arts in 1960 and a Bachelor of Education in 1962, both from the University of Manitoba, Winnipeg, Manitoba. His professional affiliations include the Royal Canadian Academy of Arts, the Print and Drawing Council of Canada, the Malaspina Printmakers Society, and the Graphics Society of New Hampshire, and he is a trustee of the Art Gallery of Brant, Brantford, Ontario.

Esler has received an impressive number of awards; the most recent are a purchase award, *3 Biennale Internationale de l'image*, Epinol, France, 1976; a purchase award, *Centennial Graphics Exhibition*, Winnipeg Art Gallery, Winnipeg, Manitoba, 1974; and a purchase award, *Canadian Society of Graphic Art Annual Exhibition,*

1974. His work is housed in many civic galleries and corporate and university collections across Canada, as well as in the Museum of Modern Art, New York; the Victoria and Albert Museum, London, England; the Canada Council Art Bank, Ottawa, Ontario; the Alberta Art Foundation, Edmonton; and the National Gallery of Canada, Ottawa, Ontario. His work is also contained in the Canadian Consulates in Cleveland, Ohio; Boston, Massachusetts; Bordeaux, France; and Port of Prince, Haiti; and in the Canadian Embassy in Guatemala. Esler has acted as a juror for several national graphics exhibitions, as well as a consulting juror for the Canada Council. Esler has participated in an impressive number of juried and invitational exhibitions, both nationally and internationally. Recent exhibitions include *Graphex 6*, the Art Gallery of Brant,

Brantford, Ontario, 1978; the *Archives Collection of the Society of Canadian Painters, Etchers, and Engravers*, Art Gallery of Hamilton, Hamilton, Ontario, 1978; *Laing, Sawai, Esler*, Graphica, Edmonton, 1978; and the *15th Anniversary Exhibition*, Gallery Pascal, Toronto, Ontario, 1978. One-person shows in 1978 were held at the Guild Gallery, Calgary; Zacks Gallery, Toronto, Ontario; Aaron Gallery, Waterloo, Ontario; and Gallery Moos, Toronto, Ontario.

Esler produces both abstract and landscape-based prints, often with social and political satirical content. He is best known for his intaglio prints, as well as his photo-etching technique.

John K. Esler is an associate professor with the Department of Art, the University of Calgary, Calgary, Alberta.

Title and date Tent III 1977
Medium colour intaglio
Size 60.5 cm x 45.5 cm

William Laing

Born in Glasgow, Scotland, in 1944, William Laing graduated from the Vancouver School of Art, Vancouver, British Columbia, with a Diploma in Photography and Printmaking in 1971. In 1971 and 1972 he studied at the Brighton Polytechnic, Brighton, England, and he received a Master of Fine Arts from the Royal College of Art, London, England, in 1974.

Laing has been the recipient of several awards, including Canada Packers Award for Printmaking, 1970; Vancouver Foundation Scholarship, 1971 to 1973; and Canada Council grants in 1973, 1975, 1976, 1977, and 1979. Collections containing Laing's work are the Museum of Art, Strasbourg, France; the National Gallery of Canada, Ottawa, Ontario; Canada House, London, England; Saidye Bronfman Centre, Montreal, Quebec; Die Treppe Gallery, Germany; and university and corporate collections in Canada, the United States, and England. Recent group exhibitions are *Selections*, the Glenbow-Alberta Institute, Calgary, 1977; *Albertawork*, the Alberta College of Art and the University of Calgary, Calgary, 1977; *Foot Print*, Davidson Gallery, Seattle, Washington, 1977; the *7th International Print Biennale*, Krakow, Poland, 1978; *Surrealism in Canadian Art*, Queen's University, Kingston, Ontario, 1978; *Graphex 7*, Art Gallery of Brant, Brantford, Ontario, 1979; and *Mednarodni Graficni Biennale*, Ljubljana, Yugoslavia, 1979.

William Laing works in lithography, etching, and silk-screen. As well as experimenting with these printmaking techniques, he draws on paper, often using an airbrush. Airbrushing may also be found on his multi-media, three-dimensional constructions. His interests lie mainly in the portrayal of the concepts of light, space, and emotion and in the documentation of his surroundings.

Laing can be reached at 76 Chancellor Way NW, Calgary, Alberta.

Title and date Coming Down #1 1977
Medium ink drawing on paper
Size 56.3 cm x 76.5 cm

Don Mabie

Don Mabie was born in Calgary in 1947 and studied both advertising art and fine art at the Alberta College of Art, Calgary. Postgraduate studies were done at the Instituto Allende, Mexico, 1970. He also studied journalism at the Southern Alberta Institute of Technology, Calgary, 1976-77. Mabie has been very active in the art community in the Calgary area and has written for several art publications in Canada. He has also founded art organizations such as the Chuck Stake Enterprises, for correspondence art (art produced on forms of mail), and the Parachute Center for Cultural Affairs in Calgary. He is the director and curator of Clouds & Water Gallery, Calgary.

Don Mabie received a Commonwealth Games Visual Arts Project Grant to produce a major work based on the Commonwealth Games, Edmonton, in 1978. As well as many exhibition awards, Mabie has received a Canada Council Arts Bursary, 1970-71; a Canada Council Travel Grant, 1971; a Province of Ontario Council for the Arts Grant to organize the *First Annual Toronto Correspondence and Junk Mail Art Exhibition*, 1974; and a Local Initiatives Program Project Grant to publish *Images and Information sort of an art magazine*, 1975. His work can be found in major collections in Alberta, British Columbia, Manitoba, and Ontario. Mabie has completed commissions such as Multipax Oxfam Editions Peace Card for Oxfam of Canada, 1971, and a poster for the Institute on Canadian Society for the University of Calgary, 1974. He has shown widely in exhibitions since 1969, including *Chuck Stake's Greatest Hits*, a one-man exhibition at the Parachute Center, Calgary, 1976; *Armpit of the Nation Postcard Show*, Gallery 25, Fresno, California, 1976; *Art in the Street*, Condurga Gallery, Madrid, Spain, 1976; *Albertawork*, University of Calgary and the Alberta College of Art, Calgary, 1977.

Mabie draws in various media such as india ink, acrylic paint, and coloured pencil. Most of his work is small in size, although he produces one or two very large pieces a year. Mabie is involved in correspondence art and participates in numerous correspondence art exhibitions throughout the world.

He can be reached at 4236 Worcester Drive SW, Calgary, Alberta.

Title and date Such is Life 1977
Medium mixed media
Size 50 cm x 60 cm

Annemarie Schmid Esler

Annemarie Schmid Esler was born in Winnipeg, Manitoba, in 1937. Her education was received at the University of Manitoba, Winnipeg, Manitoba; the University of Munich, Germany; the Alberta College of Art, Calgary; and the Archie Bray Foundation, Helena, Montana.

Awards include purchase awards in several exhibitions; Alberta Government craft scholarships, 1966, 1967, and 1968; a Canada Council Material Aid Grant, 1968; and a Manitoba Arts Council Award, the Winnipeg Art Gallery, 1976. Esler is represented in the collections of the Alberta Art Foundation, Edmonton; the Canada Council Art Bank, Ottawa, Ontario; Alberta House, London, England; the Embassy of China, Ottawa, Ontario; the House of Ceramics, Vancouver, British Columbia; and university collections in Alberta. One-person exhibitions were held at the Alberta College of Art, Calgary, 1968; Canadian Galleries, Calgary, 1970; Fleet Gallery, Winnipeg, Manitoba, 1971; Dandelion Gallery, Calgary, 1976; and the University of Calgary Gallery, 1978. Esler has also been a participant in many group exhibitions, including *The History of Ceramics in Alberta*, the Edmonton Art Gallery, Edmonton, 1975; *The Midwestern*, the Winnipeg Art Gallery, Winnipeg, Manitoba, 1976; *8 From Calgary*, the House of Ceramics, Vancouver, British Columbia, 1977; *The Fine Art of Alberta Craft*, the XI Commonwealth Games, Edmonton, 1978; and *Fifteen Canadian Artists*, Canada House, London, England, and Centre Culture, Paris, France, 1980.

Esler works in clay. The surfaces of her pieces have always been of great importance to the artist, and many materials and techniques are combined to develop the image, including the use of pencils, airbrushes, stencils, decals, and photo transfers. Landscape has always played an integral role. Both the three-dimensional landscape pieces and the large wall plates retain delicate glazes and the organic, painterly approach to the surface.

Annemarie Schmid Esler can be contacted through the mail at Box 2, Site 7, S.S.1, Calgary, Alberta.

Title and date untitled 1977
Medium clay, glaze, paper transfers
Size 53 cm (diameter)

Alexandra Haeseker

Alexandra Haeseker was born in 1945 in Breda, Holland, and moved to Canada in 1955. She received a Bachelor of Arts from the University of Calgary, 1966; a Diploma in Fine Arts from the Alberta College of Art, Calgary, 1968; and a master's degree from the University of Calgary, 1972. Since August 1973 Haeseker has been an instructor at the Alberta College of Art, Calgary.

Awards include a Canada Council grant, 1972, 1975, and 1978; Agnes Etherington Centre Award, Kingston, Ontario, 1972; Cultural Assistance Grants, Visual Arts Alberta, 1967 and 1968; as well as several purchase awards. Haeseker's work can be found in the Canada Council Art Bank, Ottawa, Ontario; the Edmonton Art Gallery, Edmonton; the Montreal Museum of Fine Art, Montreal, Quebec; Alberta House, London, England; the Alberta Art Foundation, Edmonton; and university and corporate collections throughout Canada. Haeseker has exhibited widely throughout Canada since 1968. One-person shows include the Glenbow-Alberta Institute, Calgary, 1970; Ring House Gallery, the University of Alberta, Edmonton, 1971; Marquis Gallery, the University of Saskatachewan, Saskatoon, Saskatchewan, 1971; Galerie Godard Lefort, Montreal, Quebec, 1972; and Mira Godard, Toronto, Ontario, 1978. Recent group exhibitions in which she has participated have been *What's New*, the Edmonton Art Gallery, Edmonton, 1976; *Western Untitled*, Glenbow-Alberta Institute, Calgary, 1976; *Albertawork*, the Alberta College of Art, Calgary, 1977; *Graphex 7*, the Art Gallery of Brant, Brantford, Ontario, 1979; and the *8th International Triennial of Original Coloured Graphic Prints*, the Grenchen Art Society, Haldenschulhaus, Switzerland, 1979.

Haeseker uses a variety of media with a corresponding range in scale. Large-scale canvases, approximately 163 cm x 203 cm, incorporate a combination of acrylic paint, drawing materials, and polyester casting resin to bring portions of the imagery out in relief. Medium-sized works, 76 cm x 102 cm, are collage-type drawings, involving drawing materials and resin or plexiglass. She also produces smaller watercolours and hand lithographs, generally 56 cm x 76 cm, as well as the occasional three-dimensional piece cast in polyester resin from clay originals. Haeseker's working process always begins with drawing, first and foremost. All images, whether in prints or in paintings, are hand drawn. Figures emerge as realistic fragments suspended in a fluid semi-abstract space, usually created by a loose application of washes. The same effect is created in her collages by the actual separation between figure and ground and in her paintings through the use of resin which physically advances the figure beyond the implied space.

Haeseker's home and studio address is Box 520, Midnapore, Alberta.

Title and date Late in the Day 1979
Medium mixed media on canvas
Size 162 cm x 218 cm

Charles Hilton

Charles Hilton was born in Melville, Saskatchewan, in 1937. He attended the University of Manitoba, Winnipeg, Manitoba, between the years 1958 and 1963, where he studied sculpture and pottery. In 1969 he moved to Edmonton and opened a studio. He taught pottery and sculpture for the Faculty of Extension at the University of Alberta, Edmonton, 1969 to 1971, and he was the founding director of the 1978 Commonwealth Games Sculpture Symposium.

Hilton received the Kenneth Finkelstein Prize in Sculpture from the University of Manitoba, Winnipeg, Manitoba, in 1963 and a Canada Council grant in 1970. His work can be found in private collections internationally and in public collections in Alberta, including the Alberta Art Foundation, Edmonton. Since he moved to Edmonton in 1969, Hilton has been represented in group exhibitions such as *International Ceramics 73*, Calgary, 1973; *Alberta Art Foundation Exhibition*, Japan, 1974 and 1979; and *Edmonton Clay Works*, Latitude 53 Gallery, Edmonton, 1979. Solo shows were held at the Edmonton Art Gallery, Edmonton, 1972; Graphica Gallery, Edmonton, 1978, 1979, and 1980; and Maples Gallery, Victoria, British Columbia, 1979.

Hilton is now devoting his energy to producing large-scale works conceived in clay or plaster and later cast into bronze. He also carves in wood and marble. His work is organic in form and the tactile source for the surface of his sculpture is greatly influenced by his pottery. Hilton's pottery is functional in design and includes vases and planters.

Charles Hilton may be contacted at his studio at 6910-82 Avenue, Edmonton, Alberta.

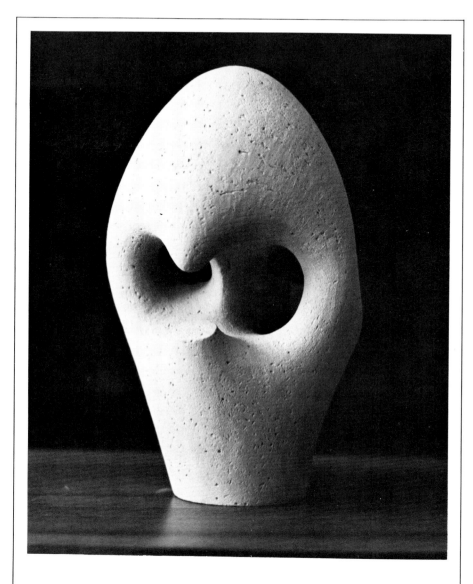

Title and date Friendship 1979
Medium plaster maquette
Size 3.6 m x 2.1 m x 2.1 m

George Angliss

George Angliss was born in 1921 in Penticton, British Columbia. He was educated at the Ontario College of Art, Toronto, Ontario, and the Vancouver School of Art, Vancouver, British Columbia. A painting instructor at the Alberta College of Art, Calgary, Angliss has had varied design experience from professionally designing for theatrical and architectural purposes to designing for advertising agencies. Angliss has been working and teaching in Alberta for the past twenty-two years.

He received a Canada Council Travel Grant in 1968 and has work in the following permanent collections: the Fathers of Confederation Art Gallery, Charlottetown, Prince Edward Island; London Public Library and Museum, London, Ontario; Mendel Art Gallery, Saskatoon, Saskatchewan; Alberta House, London, England; and the Glenbow-Alberta Institute, Calgary; as well as several corporate collections. He has exhibited widely across Canada and since 1966 has held three one-person shows which travelled nationally. He was also represented in *Albertawork*, at the University of Calgary Gallery and the Alberta College of Art Gallery, Calgary, 1977.

He has often worked with mixed-media sculptural forms as well as with paint on paper and on canvas. Subject matter includes landscapes, portraits, genre, and figure studies. He is currently producing a series of studies in high realism. Winter months are spent teaching, and he and his wife, Kay Angliss, are presently in the process of building a summer studio in the mountains of British Columbia.

Angliss works at his studio at 2428 Udell Road NW, Calgary, Alberta.

Title and date Gilby Store 1977
Medium oil on canvas
Size 70 cm x 85.5 cm

Noboru Sawai

Noboru Sawai was born in Japan in 1931 and emigrated to the United States in 1950. He received a Bachelor of Fine Arts from Augsburg College, Minneapolis, Minnesota, and a Master of Fine Arts from the University of Minnesota. In 1970 he returned to Tokyo for post-graduate study in woodcut printmaking at the Yoshida International Hanga Academy.

Since 1970 Sawai has been the recipient of several grants and awards, the most recent of which are a purchase award, the *Annual Exhibition of the Canadian Society of Graphic Art*, London, Ontario, 1974; an edition award, *Graphex 3*, Brantford, Ontario, 1975; and a junior membership award, Japan Printmakers' Association, Tokyo, Japan, 1977. He teaches with the Department of Art, the University of Calgary. Sawai's work can be found in numerous permanent collections in Canada, England, and the United States. Sawai has held over twenty one-person shows in Canada, Europe, and the United States since 1966: Mitake Gallery, Tokyo, Japan, 1979; Gallery Graphics, Ottawa, Ontario, 1978; the University of Calgary, Calgary, 1978; and Alfermann Gallery, Solingen-Ohligs, Germany, 1977. He has also exhibited extensively in competitions and group shows, both national and international, including the *47th Japan Printmakers' Annual Exhibition*, Tokyo, Japan, 1979; *3rd Graphic Biennale*, Vienna, Austria, 1977; and *Biennale International Open Competition*, Philadelphia, 1977.

Sawai's prints are the combination of woodcut and copper etching techniques. He feels that woodcuts offer fresh colour and subtle effects while the clarity of etching on copper plates reinforces the visual statement. His complex imagery is unique in the juxtaposition of traditional Japanese subject matter with images of Western civilization. The content is both erotic and humorous in its expression of the artist's physical and mental involvement with both the occidental and the oriental cultures.

Sawai's studio is at 504, 118-8 Avenue SE, Calgary, Alberta.

Title and date Matrimony 1973
Medium etching with wood block
Size 52 cm x 65.1 cm

John Chalke

Born in Gloucestershire, England, John Chalke received art training and a teacher's certificate in art education from the Bath Academy of Art, Bath, England, 1959-60. After having taught ceramics as a sessional instructor at several English art colleges, Chalke moved to Canada in 1968. He now lives in Calgary and teaches at the University of Calgary and the Alberta College of Art, Calgary.

He has received awards at the *Craft Dimensions* exhibition, Toronto, 1969; *Canadian Ceramics*, Vancouver, 1969; and *Canadian Ceramics*, Toronto, 1971; and he received a Design Canada Craft Award, Ottawa, 1974. Photographs and articles on his work have appeared in several international publications, and his work can be found in private collections throughout Canada, England, the United States, Australia, Japan, and Italy. Chalke has given workshops in ceramics and design across Canada and has participated in *Ceramic Symposia* and several juried exhibitions, including *The Fine Art of Alberta Craft*, the XI Commonwealth Games, Edmonton, 1978, and the *IV International Ceramics Exhibition*, Gdansk, Poland, 1979. He collaborated with Wengers Ceramic Supplies of Stoke upon Trent, England, to develop clays, glazes, and equipment for educational institutions and has exhibited in Canada, England, Switzerland, Italy, the United States, and Denmark.

Characteristics of pottery from the past and the present can be found in Chalke's current work. His main sources are Japanese pottery from the Momoyama period and pottery from Medieval England. He considers himself to be a clay glazer, and a painterly glaze application is used to heighten the tactile qualities of his work. For the past seven years he has been experimenting with free-form rather than wheel-thrown ceramics, although he still creates what he calls country pots based on a more traditional approach to potting techniques.

Chalke's home and studio address is 429-12 Street NW, Calgary, Alberta.

Title and date untitled 1976
Medium clay, glazed
Size 53 cm (diameter) x 5 cm (approximately)

Carroll Moppett

Carroll Moppett was born in Calgary in 1948. She attended the Alberta College of Art, Calgary, 1966-67 and 1974-75, and the Instituto Allende, Mexico, 1968. Between 1967 and 1969 she was employed by the Arts and Crafts Division, Department of Culture, Youth, and Recreation, Government of Alberta.

Moppett received a Canada Council Arts Grant in 1978 and held a solo exhibition at the University of Calgary, 1976, and at Artons, Calgary, 1978. Group exhibitions in which she has participated include *Contemporary Ceramic Sculpture*, the University of British Columbia, Vancouver, 1974; *The History of Ceramics in Alberta*, the Edmonton Art Gallery, Edmonton, and the Alberta College of Art, Calgary, 1975; *Spectrum Canada*, Royal Canadian Academy National Exhibition, Montreal, Quebec, 1976; *Albertawork*, the University of Calgary and the Alberta College of Art, Calgary, 1977; *Obsessions Rituals Controls*, Norman Mackenzie Art Gallery, Regina, Saskatchewan, 1978; and *Alberta Works in Wood*, Alberta College of Art Gallery, Calgary, 1979.

Moppett uses many different materials, including canvas and wood. She has stated that her process is based on a conscious interest in form. These forms are achieved through the artist's innate concern with landscape and shaminism. She is involved with the emotive quality of form, and the size of her work ranges from small pieces to those somewhat larger than human scale.

Carroll Moppett lives at 319-11 Street NW, Calgary, Alberta.

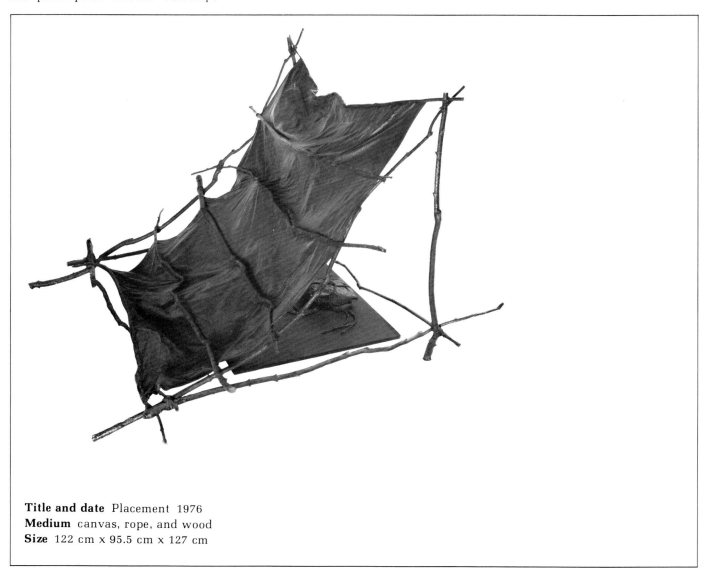

Title and date Placement 1976
Medium canvas, rope, and wood
Size 122 cm x 95.5 cm x 127 cm

Glenn Guillet

Glenn Guillet was born in 1949 in Prince Rupert, British Columbia. He graduated from the University of Alberta, Edmonton, in 1971, with a Bachelor of Fine Arts. He is now a part-time instructor at the University of Alberta's Faculty of Extension in Edmonton.

In 1976 he received a Canada Council Project Grant. His work may be found in the collection of the Alberta Art Foundation, Edmonton. Since his graduation from university in 1971, Guillet has held five one-person exhibitions: Edmonton Art Gallery, Edmonton, 1973; Latitude 53 Gallery, Edmonton, 1975, 1977, and 1978; and SUB Gallery, University of Alberta, Edmonton, 1980. He was also represented in *West '71*, the Edmonton Art Gallery, Edmonton, 1971; *What's New*, the Edmonton Art Gallery, Edmonton, 1976; and *Circa '76 Sculpture*, Latitude 53 Gallery, Edmonton, 1977.

Guillet usually works in chrome, and the majority of the sculptures he has completed within the last five years have been based on the effects of the motion of optically perfect forms. A motor located in the base of each work slowly rotates the sculpture so that the chrome surface reflects the environment; thus the sculpture seems to undulate with an energy of its own. The sculpture is connected to an electric eye which activates it whenever a viewer is present. Guillet also draws in coloured crayon on paper.

Glenn Guillet can be reached at 11127-82 Avenue, Edmonton, Alberta.

Title and date Solid Tide 1976
Medium chrome, motorized
Size 30 cm x 28 cm x 28 cm

David Dorrance

David Dorrance was born in 1946 in Sault Ste. Marie, Ontario. He attended State University of New York College, Brockport, New York, and graduated from the University of Wisconsin, Madison, Wisconsin, with a Master of Fine Arts in 1975. He has taught at the Alberta College of Art, Calgary; Kansas State University, Manhattan, Kansas; the University of Wisconsin, Madison, Wisconsin; and the University of Regina, Regina, Saskatchewan.

Dorrance's work has been purchased by the Canada Council Art Bank, Ottawa, and he has been exhibiting regularly across the United States and in Western Canada since 1971. Selected exhibitions include *100 Artists Commemorate 200 Years*, Fairtree Gallery, New York, New York, 1976; the *National Sculpture Competitive Exhibition*, Corpus Christi, Texas, 1976; the *Canadian National Ceramics Exhibition*, Glenbow-Alberta Institute, Calgary, 1977; *Souvenirs: One Man Exhibition*, Dandelion Gallery, Calgary, 1977; *No Dogs in Parks: Solo Exhibition*, California State University, Hayward, California, 1978; and *3 Works: Solo Exhibition*, University of Wisconsin, Madison, Wisconsin, 1979.

Dorrance began working in clay in 1970. His interest in casting led him to other materials—paper, latex rubber, and polyester resin—suitable for use in molds. Several cast reproductions of objects are combined in his finished work or contemporary still life. His main concern is with the assembling of these reproduced objects and with their interaction. Surfaces are treated with a combination of glazes and paints.

David Dorrance can be contacted c/o Dandelion Gallery, 806-9 Avenue SE, Calgary, Alberta.

Title and date Yardbird 1977
Medium ceramic, paint
Size 114 cm x 43 cm x 21 cm

Norman Faulkner

Born in Edmonton in 1944, Norman Faulkner graduated from the Alberta College of Art, Calgary, in 1973. He has taught ceramics and glass blowing at the Alberta College of Art, Calgary, since 1974.

Faulkner received the Prize for Glass, Kingston Olympic Committee, 1976, and a Canada Council grant, for glass study, 1972. Faulkner has been represented in several group shows nationally, including *Hand to Hand*, Kingston Olympics Exhibit, Kingston, Ontario, 1976; *The History of Ceramics in Alberta*, the Edmonton Art Gallery, Edmonton, 1975; *Canadian Glass*, House of Ceramics Gallery, Vancouver, British Columbia, 1977; *8 From Calgary*, House of Ceramics Gallery, Vancouver, British Columbia, 1977; *The Fine Art of Alberta Craft*, the XI Commonwealth Games, Edmonton, 1978; and *The Works*, SUB Gallery, the University of Alberta, Edmonton, 1979. Solo shows were held at the Alberta College of Art Gallery, Calgary, in 1971 and 1973, as well as Dandelion Gallery, Calgary, in 1976.

Faulkner's background is predominately in ceramics. However, for the past few years he has been working almost exclusively in glass. "Besides being well suited to my current interests in form and surface, the immediacy of the glass-blowing process makes it an ideal pursuit for an artist whose time is regimented by full-time teaching duties." His more elaborate pieces combine different forming techniques such as blowing and casting.

Norman Faulkner lives at 1408 Gladstone Road NW, Calgary, Alberta. He may also be reached through the Alberta College of Art, 1301-16 Avenue NW, Calgary, Alberta.

Title and date untitled 1977
Medium offhand blown glass
Size 27 cm (height)

Robert Guest

obert Guest was born in 1938 in Beaverlodge, Alberta. In 1956 and 1957 he was awarded scholarships to summer-school courses at the Banff Centre School of Fine Arts. He is a graduate of the Alberta College of Art, Calgary, 1963, and the University of Alberta, Edmonton, 1974. He is now on the staff of the Grande Prairie Regional College, where he co-ordinates the Art Department, the first in the Peace River area. Robert Guest was also one of the nine founding members of the Alberta Art Foundation established by the provincial government. As a result of his interest in nature and conservation he founded the Canadian Wolf Defenders society and Wil Kakwa, the first conservation society of the Peace River country.

Guest exhibits mainly in northern Alberta and in Edmonton. He may take up to one and one-half months to complete a pen-and-ink drawing. Nature continues to be Guest's primary source of inspiration. "Traditionally it seems that much landscape has been confused with a calendar trend. While a good painting or drawing can serve both purposes, to me it should go deeper than that. On the one hand, the artist is a scientist observing natural phenomena, and, on the other, an inventor." His challenge is finding a balance between these two extremes.

Although best known for his pen-and-ink drawings, Guest also experiments with watercolour and oils. Recently he combined black ink with brown, resulting in what he labels a coppertone technique.

Robert Guest's address is 10812-104 Street, Grande Prairie, Alberta.

Title and date Indian Graves #7 1974
Medium ink on paper
Size 23 cm x 15.5 cm

Marcella Bienvenue

Marcella Bienvenue was born in Stettler, Alberta, in 1946. She graduated from the Alberta College of Art, Calgary, in 1969.

In 1968 she received the H. Jordon Memorial Scholarship, as well as an Alberta Visual Arts Scholarship. Other awards include a purchase award from the *7th Burnaby Print Show*, Burnaby, British Columbia, 1973, and a Canada Council Project Cost Grant, 1975. Bienvenue's work has been acquired by several permanent collections such as the Alberta Art Foundation, Edmonton; the Canada Council Art Bank, Ottawa, Ontario; the Burnaby Art Gallery, Burnaby, British Columbia; Alberta House, London, England; and several corporate collections. Since her graduation in 1969, Bienvenue has participated in a minimum of two group shows per year, including *2 Woman—2 Man Show*, Latitude 53 Gallery, Edmonton, 1975; *Woman as Viewer*, Winnipeg Art Gallery, Winnipeg, Manitoba, 1975; *Through the Looking Glass Toward a New Reality*, Art Gallery of Ontario, Toronto, Ontario, 1975; *Imprint '76*, Montreal Museum of Fine Arts, Montreal, Quebec, 1976; and *Works on Paper*, the Alberta College of Art Gallery, Calgary, 1976.

Between 1971 and 1975 Bienvenue worked primarily with the photographic silk-screen process. In early 1976 she became aware of the possibilities of the commercial off-set litho, as it offered photographic clarity of image and greater production speed. She is interested in establishing off-set lithography as a recognized art print medium.

Marcella Bienvenue can be reached at 1139-6 Avenue SW, Calgary, Alberta.

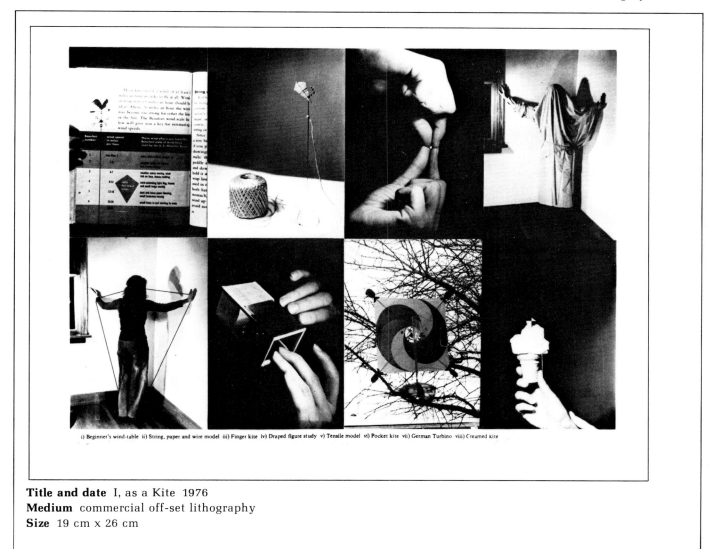

i) Beginner's wind-table ii) String, paper and wire model iii) Finger kite iv) Draped figure study v) Tensile model vi) Pocket kite vii) German Turbino viii) Creamed kite

Title and date I, as a Kite 1976
Medium commercial off-set lithography
Size 19 cm x 26 cm

Liz Gagnon

Liz Gagnon was born in Argentina in 1949 and has been a resident of Alberta since 1974. A Master of Visual Arts graduate from the University of Alberta, Edmonton, Gagnon also studied at York University, Toronto, Ontario. She is now a sessional lecturer in printmaking with the Department of Art and Design at the University of Alberta, Edmonton.

Gagnon received an Award of Merit for a Young Professional and a purchase award at *Graphex 6*, the Art Gallery of Brant, Brantford, Ontario, 1978. Collections containing her work are the Government of Alberta, Edmonton; the Canada Council Art Bank, Ottawa, Ontario; Owens Art Gallery, Sackville, New Brunswick; and the Universities of Oregon, Alberta, and Guelph. Gagnon has exhibited in such shows as *Imprint '76*, Saidye Bronfman Center, Montreal, Quebec, 1976; *7th International Print Biennale*, Krakow, Poland, 1978; *Intergraphia '78*, Katowice, Poland, 1978; and *Graphex 7*, the Art Gallery of Brant, Brantford, Ontario, 1979. She was represented in a three-person exhibition at the Hong Kong Arts Centre, Hong Kong, 1979, and held a solo exhibition of prints and drawings at Gallery Pascal, Toronto, Ontario, 1979.

Gagnon is primarily interested in combining various printmaking techniques such as photo-lithography and serigraphy. The photographic imagery is taken from parts of the body and elements of plant life. She considers the relationship between the direct mark-making of brush on lithography plate and the photographic image to be the major emphasis in her work.

Liz Gagnon can be contacted at her home address of 9823-90 Avenue, Edmonton, Alberta, or through the Department of Art and Design, the University of Alberta, Edmonton, Alberta.

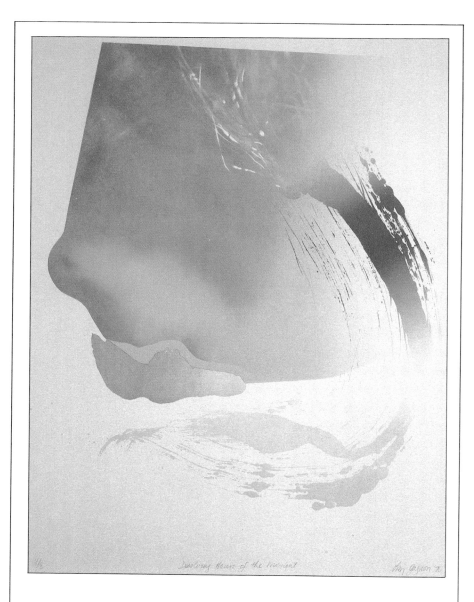

Title and date Dissolving Hours of the Moment 1977
Medium litho/screen print
Size 94.5 cm x 72.5 cm

68

Derek Rodgers

Born in England in 1939, Derek Rodgers graduated from the Alberta College of Art, Calgary, with a major in printmaking.

Awards include a study grant from the City of Calgary, 1973, and a graduation scholarship from the Alberta College of Art, Calgary, 1973. Collections containing his work are the Alberta Art Foundation, Edmonton;

Alberta House, London, England; and the University of British Columbia, Vancouver, British Columbia. Exhibitions include two-person shows in both Calgary and Vancouver. Rodgers was represented in *Albertawork*, at the University of Calgary and the Alberta College of Art, Calgary, 1977, as well as various local exhibitions. In 1976 he held a one-person show at Galerie Royale, Vancouver.

Rodgers experiments with many graphic techniques, including stone lithography, linoleum block printing, and drawing. His drawings are usually oil and chalk pastels or graphite combined with crayon on paper. He has also worked in collage.

He can be reached at his home address of 1345 Colgrove Avenue NE, Calgary, Alberta.

Title and date Rocky Mountain Fantasia 1977
Medium mixed-media collage
Size 50.5 cm x 65.5 cm

Dennis Evans

Dennis Evans was born in 1942 in Hamilton, Ohio. He received a Bachelor of Fine Arts from the Cleveland Institute of Art, Cleveland, Ohio, in 1968 and a Master of Fine Arts from the University of North Carolina, Greensboro, North Carolina, in 1971. At present he is an instructor with the Sculpture Department at the Alberta College of Art, Calgary.

Evans was awarded a Page Award from the Cleveland Institute of Art, Cleveland, Ohio, in 1967 and a grant from the Southern Alberta Institute of Technology, Calgary, to attend the International Institute of Experimental Printmaking, Santa Cruz, California, in 1976. Collections containing Evans's work are Alberta Government House, Edmonton; the Alberta Art Foundation, Edmonton; the Art Gallery of Brant, Brantford, Ontario; and the Southern Alberta Institute of Technology, Calgary. Evans's sculpture was shown in the following exhibitions: *Albertawork*, the Alberta College of Art and the University of Calgary, Calgary, 1977; *Sculpture on the Prairies*, the Winnipeg Art Gallery, Winnipeg, Manitoba, 1977; *Graphex 7*, the Art Gallery of Brant, Brantford, Ontario, 1979; and *Fifteen*, the Walter Phillips Gallery, Banff, Alberta, 1979.

Evans has had experience with a variety of materials and equipment—foundry techniques including bronze and aluminum casting; mold-making with plaster, rubber, and fibreglass; welding; carving in wood, stone, and polystyrene foam; ceramics; and handmade papers. His work does not depend on any particular media but, rather, is a combination of materials and experimental processes. His target works, involving the ever-changing visual images created through the discipline of archery, are documentations of a year and one-half of work. These archery pieces are closely related to the performance work with which Evans has been experimenting for the last four years.

Dennis Evans can be contacted through the Alberta College of Art, 1301-16 Avenue NW, Calgary, Alberta.

Title and date Missing the Ten Spot is Indicative of One's Life 1977
Medium aluminum arrows, target, and butt
Size 120 cm x 90 cm x 75 cm

Patrick Hurst

Patrick Hurst was born in Vulcan, Alberta, in 1947. He received a Bachelor of Arts and a Bachelor of Fine Arts from the University of Calgary, as well as a Bachelor of Architecture from the University of British Columbia, Vancouver. He received a Master of Arts from the University of Saskatchewan, Saskatoon, Saskatchewan.

Awards include a Province of Alberta, Cultural Branch, Visual Arts Award, in 1967; Continuing Arts Association Calgary Scholarship, 1972; Major Arts Award, Saskatchewan Arts Board, Regina, Saskatchewan; Canada Council Project Cost Award, 1979; and several purchase awards. His work is housed in the Alberta Art Foundation, Edmonton; the University of Calgary Permanent Collection, Calgary; the Art Gallery of Brant, Brantford, Ontario; the Canada Council Art Bank, Ottawa, Ontario; and the University of Saskatchewan, Saskatoon, Saskatchewan. Patrick Hurst has held one-person exhibitions at the Mount Royal College Art Gallery, Calgary, 1976, and the Shoestring Gallery, Saskatoon, Saskatchewan, 1979. His graphics were shown at *Graphex 4, 5, 6,* and *7,* the Art Gallery of Brant, Brantford, Ontario, 1976, 1977, 1978, and 1979, and shows containing his sculptures include *Albertawork,* the University of Calgary and the Alberta College of Art, Calgary, 1977; *8 From Calgary,* House of Ceramics, Vancouver, British Columbia, 1977; and *Alberta and Ontario Potters Guild,* Toronto, Ontario, 1978.

Hurst's subject matter deals with heroes and anti-heroes. He likes to explore the same theme or similar ideas in both two and three dimensions. His two-dimensional work is mainly in the area of lithography and mixed-media drawing. His three-dimensional pieces are porcelain sculptures, brightly glazed and often incorporating molds from various children's toys.

Hurst can be reached at 313-7 Avenue NE, Calgary, Alberta.

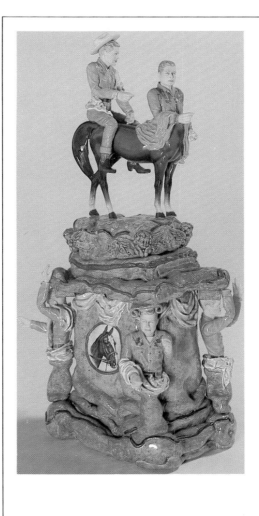

Title and date Equestrian Statue of Johnny West 1977
Medium porcelain, glazed
Size 62 cm x 32 cm x 24 cm

Gordon Ferguson

Gordon Ferguson was born in High River, Alberta, in 1953. He graduated from the Alberta College of Art, Calgary, in 1976 and from the University of Montana, Missoula, Montana, with a Bachelor of Fine Arts in 1979.

Ferguson's sculpture can be found in the collection of Long Mayell and Associates, Calgary. He held a solo exhibition at the University Center, Missoula, Montana, 1979, and partic-ipated in *Albertawork*, the University of Calgary and the Alberta College of Art, Calgary, 1977, and the *Graduate Show*, the Alberta College of Art, Calgary, 1976.

The majority of Ferguson's sculpture is constructed in steel, although some are wood and metal combinations. His pieces range in size from two cubic metres to six cubic metres and most are made to be situated out of doors since rust and sunlight are considered important elements in the initial composition. Ferguson emphasizes simple geometric shapes in his sculpture. Thus, wood and metal are preferred for their straight-edge properties. He also produces drawings in chalk, charcoal washes, and pencil, which he considers as blueprints for his three-dimensional work.

Gordon Ferguson can be reached through Box 172, Oyen, Alberta.

Title and date untitled 1976
Medium steel
Size 6 m x 4.5 m x 4.5 m

David Foxcroft

David Foxcroft was born in Calgary in 1953. He graduated in 1977 from the Alberta College of Art, Calgary, with a Diploma in Fine Arts, majoring in painting. He teaches drawing to first-year students at the Alberta College of Art, Calgary.

Foxcroft received a Canada Council grant in 1977. Since his graduation he has been represented in *Albertawork*, the University of Calgary and the Alberta College of Art, Calgary, 1977, and *Fifteen*, the Walter Phillips Gallery, Banff, 1979.

Foxcroft's mixed-media works are constructed of canvas, wood, acrylic paint, plaster, and string. Found objects are often the stimulus for his composition, and bright colour is used to emphasize the three-dimensional aspects of the construction. His pieces are assembled with objects such as ladders and bamboo poles, often projecting from hinged sections of stretched canvas.

David Foxcroft can be contacted at his home and studio address of 158 Pinehill Road NE, Calgary, Alberta, or through the Alberta College of Art, 1301-16 Avenue NW, Calgary, Alberta.

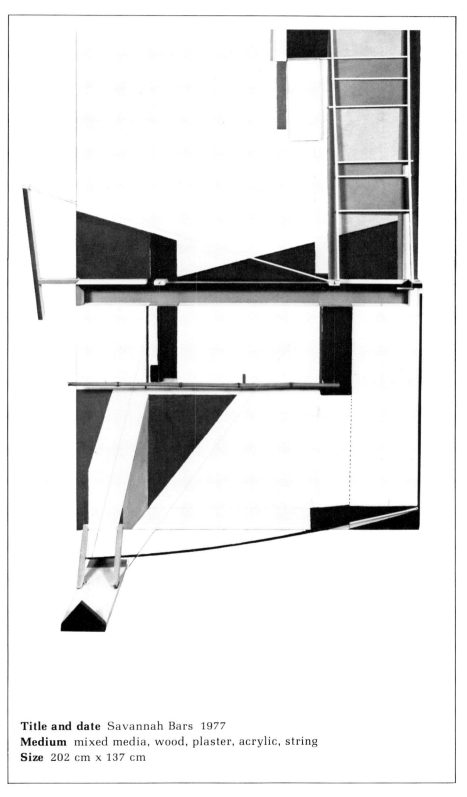

Title and date Savannah Bars 1977
Medium mixed media, wood, plaster, acrylic, string
Size 202 cm x 137 cm

William Parker

William Parker was born in Calgary in 1946. He graduated from the Alberta College of Art, Calgary, in 1972, where he taught drawing and painting between 1974 and 1977.

Parker's work hangs in the collections of the Alberta Art Foundation, Edmonton; the Department of Public Works, Edmonton; and corporate collections in Calgary. He held a solo exhibition in Canadian Galleries, Calgary, 1979, and has participated in group shows across Canada, including *Alberta Realists,* the Edmonton Art Gallery, Edmonton, 1974; the *ACA Faculty Exhibition,* the Alberta College of Art Gallery, Calgary, 1975; *4 Alberta Realists,* Latitude 53 Gallery, Edmonton, 1976; *Young Contemporaries '76,* cross-Canada travelling exhibition, 1976; and the *Alberta Society of Artists Annual Exhibition,* 1977.

Parker often uses photographs as initial reference in his work, but he discards them once the painting is further developed. He paints in acrylic and oils on fabric-covered panels which he constructs himself. Unlike many contemporary realists, he does not use egg tempera. Although a large number of his paintings deal with subject matter exhibiting a deep space, such as land and rock forms or the female figure, Parker strives "to maintain the integrity of the flat picture plane as much as possible—I try to maintain a precarious balance between the painting as an object itself and the objects from nature represented in that painting. In other words, in contrast to many of the traditional realists, I am no more concerned with subject or theme than with the art work itself."

Bill Parker can be found at Box 34, Site 13, R.R.4, Calgary, Alberta.

Title and date Sally No. 2 1977
Medium acrylic, plywood
Size 91 cm x 91 cm

George Wood

Born in Regina, Saskatchewan, in 1932, George Wood graduated from the Alberta College of Art, Calgary, 1956, and the University of Manitoba, School of Art, Winnipeg, Manitoba, 1958. Wood is now an instructor in painting and design at the Alberta College of Art, Calgary.

In 1961 Wood received the International Award at the *College Art Teachers Exhibition*, New York. He was also the recipient of the Jacox Award, *All Alberta Show*, 1964. His work is housed in many collections across Canada, including the Mendel Art Gallery, Saskatoon, Saskatchewan; the Saskatchewan Arts Board, Regina, Saskatchewan; Beaverbrook Art Gallery, Fredericton, New Brunswick; the Alberta Art Foundation, Edmonton; the London Public Library and Art Museum, London, Ontario; and in university collections across Canada. Since 1962 Wood has held ten solo exhibitions through the Western Canada Art Circuit, 1967-68; the Atlantic Provinces Art Circuit, 1967-68; the National Gallery of Canada, Ottawa, Ontario, 1968-69; and Agghazy Gallery, Calgary, 1975. He has also been represented in many group shows, including *Eleven Alberta Painters*, Art Institute of Ontario, travelling exhibition, 1961, and the *Fifth Biennal of Canadian Painting*, the National Gallery of Canada, Ottawa, Ontario, 1963-64.

Wood's paintings vary in size and are painted in acrylic or oils with an acrylic base. He is interested in the association of people with things or objects and with the relationship between the passage of time and these objects. His main concern is to portray the relevance of history, most notably that of the early twentieth century, to present times. His paintings are done in thematic groupings such as the *Flag Set* or *Ann in the 20th Century*.

Wood lives at 4340 Viscount Drive NW, Calgary, Alberta.

Title and date Flag Set No. 28—London Suite—Combined Ops. 1972
Medium acrylic on canvas
Size 155 cm x 121 cm

Walter May

Walter May was born in Edmonton in 1950 and graduated with a Bachelor of Fine Arts from the University of Alberta, Edmonton, 1971, and a Master of Fine Arts from the University of Regina, Regina, Saskatchewan, 1977.

May has received several educational scholarships as well as a travel grant from the University of Regina, 1976, and Canada Council grants in 1977 and 1978. His work may be found in the collections of the Alberta College of Art, Calgary; the University of Regina, Regina, Saskatchewan; the Alberta Art Foundation, Edmonton; Alberta Culture, Edmonton; and the Canada Council Art Bank, Ottawa, Ontario. May has exhibited in *Forum '76*, Montreal Museum of Fine Arts, Montreal, Quebec, 1976; *Sculpture on the Prairies*, the Winnipeg Art Gallery, Winnipeg, Manitoba, 1977; *Obsessions Rituals Controls*, Norman Mackenzie Art Gallery, Regina, Saskatchewan, 1978; and *Summer in the City*, Clouds & Water Gallery, Calgary, 1979. He participated in two-person exhibitions in Calgary and Banff in 1979.

Walter May has been involved with both sculpture and drawing for several years. His drawings are illusionistic tonal renderings of small objects such as twigs, stones, feathers, cigars, and rags. The actual model is mounted on the drawing or is attached to the frame. The framing of these works is becoming increasingly complex, extending out from the wall and often incorporating mirrors and exotic paint finishes. As May includes the model and develops the frame as an integral part of the piece, his drawings have become three-dimensional sculptural objects.

Walter May can be contacted at his home and studio of 1104-6 Avenue SW, Calgary, Alberta.

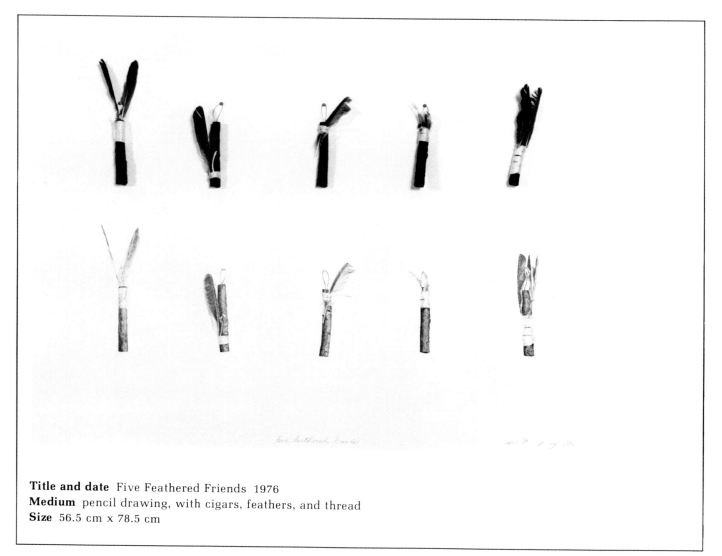

Title and date Five Feathered Friends 1976
Medium pencil drawing, with cigars, feathers, and thread
Size 56.5 cm x 78.5 cm

Lynn Mauser-Bain

Born in Oakland, California, in 1944, Lynn Mauser-Bain graduated with a Bachelor of Science from the University of Oregon, 1966, and a Master of Arts from the University of California at Berkeley, 1970. She has led workshops and instructed at the University of California at Berkeley; Portland State University, Oregon; the University of Iowa, Iowa City; the University of Oregon, Oregon; and the Alberta College of Art, Calgary. She has acted as a juror for several exhibitions, as well as having co-ordinated the *Fibre Artists Interchange,* Banff, Alberta, 1979.

She was Fulbright Scholar to Stockholm, Sweden, 1971, and was awarded the Best in Show, *Made by Hand,*

Craftsmen's Association of British Columbia Show, 1976. Permanent collections containing her work are in Government House, Edmonton, and Huddinge Sjukhus, Stockholm, Sweden. Mauser-Bain has been represented in such exhibitions as *Made by Hand,* the Craftsmen's Association of British Columbia, 1976 and 1978; *Banff Centre Faculty Exhibition,* Banff, Alberta, 1977 and 1978; the *Canada Crafts Council Touring Exhibition,* 1977 and 1978; and *Contacts,* Fibrework Symposium, Oakland, California, 1978. Solo shows were held at the Contemporary Crafts Gallery, Portland, Oregon, 1971 and 1975; the United States Cultural Centre, Stockholm, Sweden, 1972; Anneberg Gallery, San Francisco, 1974; and Kootenay School

of Art, Nelson, B.C., 1979.

Lynn Mauser-Bain works with handmade felt which she creates by pressing together dyed wool fibres. The process is conducive to any size or shape, and the dyed wool can be coloured in many shades and tones from bright to sombre. Often colours are blended together, the result being layers and flaps that reveal various colours underneath the surface. Mauser-Bain works on commission, and her felt pieces are architectural in scale, suitable for buildings and public areas. Felt is very light in weight and has very good insulation properties for both heat and sound.

She can be reached c/o 4423-37 Street NW, Calgary, Alberta.

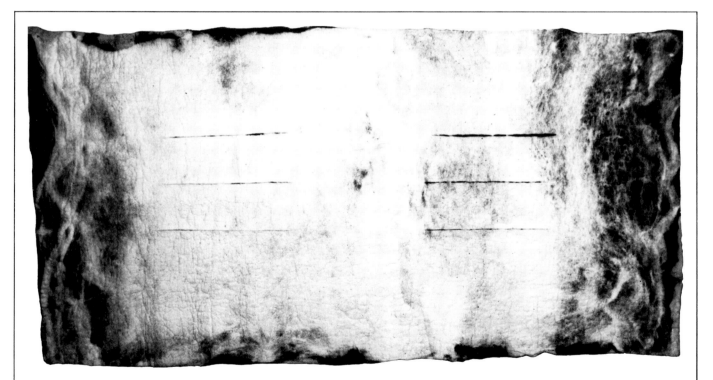

Title and date Field 1977
Medium felt
Size 187 cm x 350 cm

Kay Angliss

Kay Angliss was educated at the Vancouver School of Art and furthered her studies at the Emma Lake Workshop, the University of Saskatchewan, at the University of Calgary printmaking workshops, and through special studies at the Alberta College of Art, Calgary. She is now an art instructor at the Southern Alberta Institute of Technology in Calgary.

Her work can be found in the Alberta Art Foundation, Edmonton; Alberta House, London, England; Confederation Art Gallery and Museum, Charlottetown, Prince Edward Island; and the University of Calgary. One of Angliss's major commissions consisted of four large, coloured banners for the new Law Courts Building, Edmonton. Her work, particularly the banner constructions, has been of much interest to architects and designers. In 1972 she mounted a one-person show which travelled to eight Canadian galleries, including the Burnaby Art Gallery, British Columbia, and the Fathers of Confederation Art Gallery and Museum, Charlottetown. Group exhibitions in which she has participated were held at the Winnipeg Art Gallery, Manitoba, 1969, and Memorial University, St. John's, Newfoundland, 1970 and 1971. Her work has been exhibited in major invitational group shows in Alberta.

Kay Angliss works in several media, including fibre, serigraphy, and watercolour. Her fibre works, most notably the cloth banners, are brightly coloured constructions consisting of a wide variety of materials. Her serigraphs and collographs usually follow a theme such as the *Antique Hardware Series*. Recently, she has been working on a series of watercolour studies using landscape and figure themes.

Kay Angliss can be reached through the Southern Alberta Institute of Technology, Adult Education Department, or at home at 2428 Udell Road NW, Calgary, Alberta.

Title and date 1908 Builder's Hardware #4 1977
Medium serigraph
Size 27 cm x 38 cm

Harry Savage

Harry Savage was born in 1938 in Camrose, Alberta. He graduated from the Alberta College of Art, Calgary, in 1961 and the Brooks School of Photography, Santa Barbara, California, in 1962.

Savage has been invited to jury many exhibitions and has received several awards in exhibitions in which his work has been shown, including the Andrew McClintok Bell Award at the *Canadian Watercolour Society Show* in 1977. He also received the Edmonton Achievement Award for Arts from the City of Edmonton, 1977. His work can be found in the Edmonton Art Gallery, Edmonton; the Alberta Art Foundation, Edmonton; Shell Oil Collection, Calgary; the Glenbow Foundation, Calgary; the Burnaby Art Gallery, Burnaby, British Columbia; and several university collections. Harry Savage has been exhibiting since 1973. His work was shown in *Alberta Art Foundation Selections,* Glenbow-Alberta Institute, Calgary, 1977; *Director's Choice,* the Edmonton Art Gallery, Edmonton, 1978; and *Alberta Landscape,* the Edmonton Art Gallery, Edmonton, 1979. Savage has held solo exhibitions at the Dandelion Gallery, Calgary, 1977; Chapman Gallery, Red Deer, 1978; and the Edmonton Art Gallery, Edmonton, 1979.

Savage is primarily interested in portraying the prairie landscape in watercolour. His paintings are usually small, measuring approximately 20 cm x 30 cm. He has also painted seascape imagery, which is similar to his prairie imagery in the direct and simplified expression of the horizontal relationship between water and sky or land and sky. Besides watercolours, Savage produces photo-serigraphs, usually in a series, which are often political or environmental statements. He is a well-known photographer, and his photographs have been recently published in a book, *Alberta: A Celebration*, in which he collaborated with novelist Rudy Wiebe.

Harry Savage lives at 9820-92 Avenue, Edmonton, Alberta.

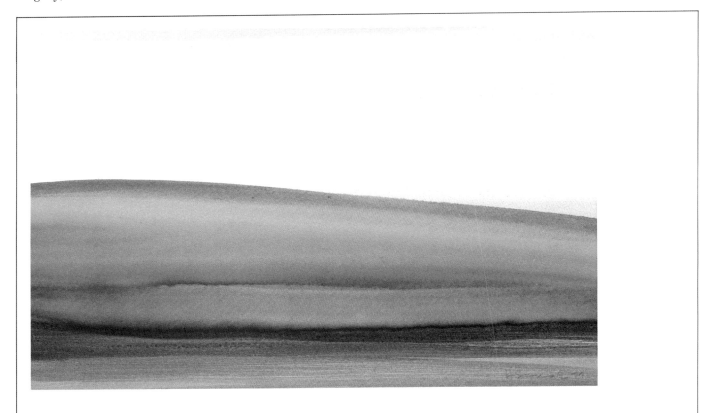

Title and date Partridge Hill Road Series 1977
Medium watercolour on paper
Size 19 cm x 29 cm

Violet Owen

Violet Owen was born in Edmonton in 1930. She has been painting in the city since her graduation from the Ontario College of Art, Toronto, Ontario, in 1953.

Owen's work can be located in the following public collections: the Edmonton Public School Board, Edmonton; the Alberta Art Foundation, Edmonton; the University of New Brunswick, Fredericton, New Brunswick; and the Edmonton Art Gallery, Edmonton. Owen has participated in over thirty-five group shows and was represented in the *Alberta Art Foundation European Exhibition,* 1975. She has held a one-person show at the University of New Brunswick Art Centre, Fredericton, New Brunswick, in 1971 and 1972, which travelled through the Atlantic Provinces Art Circuit, as well as a one-person show at the Edmonton Art Gallery, Edmonton, 1973. In total Owen has held fifteen one-person shows since 1961, the most recent of which was sponsored by the Edmonton Art Gallery, Extension Services, to tour Canada, 1977 to 1979. In 1974 and 1975 she was commissioned to execute chalk studies of Lieutenant-Governor J. Grant MacEwan and House Speaker Gerard Amerongen. The studies are now in the collection of the Government of Alberta, Edmonton.

Owen is a figurative artist and always works directly from life. She draws with black chalk or charcoal on full-size illustration board and has recently been experimenting with applying paint directly to sheets of plexiglass. Her subject matter is most often that of the female figure.

Owen works in her home and studio at 1801, 10025-113 Street, Edmonton, Alberta.

Title and date Hair 1973
Medium chalk on illustration board
Size 100 cm x 75 cm

Ihor Dmytruk

Edmonton artist Ihor Dmytruk was born in 1938 in the Ukraine. He moved to Canada in 1949 and teaches with the Faculty of Extension, University of Alberta. Dmytruk studied at the University of Alberta and the Vancouver School of Art.

He was awarded Canada Council grants in 1966, 1972, and 1974. His works are located in several major public collections, including the Canada Council Art Bank, Ottawa, Ontario; the Alberta Art Foundation, Edmonton; Government House, Edmonton; and the Ukrainian Institute of Modern Art, Chicago, Illinois. Dmytruk's one-person shows include the Edmonton Art Gallery, Edmonton, 1971; the Ukrainian Institute of Modern Art, Chicago, Illinois, 1974; and Latitude 53 Gallery, Edmonton, 1975 and 1977. Group shows include *9 Out of 10, A Survey of Contemporary Canadian Art*, Hamilton Gallery, Hamilton, Ontario, 1974; *Savage/Dmytruk*, Latitude 53 Gallery, Edmonton, 1977; *Alberta Art Foundation Selections*, Edmonton, 1978; and a group drawing show, SUB Gallery, University of Alberta, Edmonton, 1979.

Currently, Dmytruk has been working with watercolour and drawing pencil. The scale of his work ranges from minute 15 cm x 15 cm watercolours to 70 cm x 55 cm drawings. His sources include microscopic organic form and landscape. He likes to experiment within his chosen media. Although he is now producing watercolours and pencil drawings, in the past he has produced many large-scale acrylic canvases.

Ihor Dmytruk can be reached through 9803-92 Avenue, Edmonton, Alberta.

Title and date Drawing #42 1976
Medium pencil on paper
Size 56 cm x 71 cm

Takao Tanabe

Takao Tanabe was born in Prince Rupert, British Columbia, in 1926. He attended the Banff School of Fine Arts, Banff; the Brooklyn Museum Art School, Brooklyn, New York; the Winnipeg School of Art, Winnipeg, Manitoba; Hans Hofmann, New York, New York; Central School of Arts and Crafts, London, England; and Isao Hirayama, Tokyo University of Fine Arts, Tokyo, Japan. He is the head of the Painting and Sculpture Division of the Visual Arts Department at the Banff Centre School of Fine Arts, Banff.

Tanabe received a Canada Council Junior Award, 1959, and a Canada Council Senior Fellowship in 1969. He also received the Emily Carr Foundation Scholarship in 1953. Permanent collections housing his paintings consist of the National Gallery of Canada, Ottawa; Benson & Hedges, Toronto, Ontario; Toronto Dominion Bank, Toronto, Ontario; J. C. Penny, New York, New York; Canadian Council Art Bank, Ottawa, Ontario; as well as university and civic galleries in major centres in Canada and the United States. Since 1951 Tanabe's impressive exhibition history includes shows at the Guggenheim, New York, 1956; the National Gallery of Canada, Ottawa, Ontario, 1963, 1964, 1965, and 1968; the Nihonbashi Gallery, Tokyo, Japan, 1960; the Commonwealth Centre, London, England, 1962; and the Art Bank, Paris, France, 1973. One-person shows were held at the Equinox Gallery, Vancouver, British Columbia, 1975 and 1977; Marlborough-Rome, Italy, 1975; Marlborough-Godard, Montreal, Quebec, 1975; Mira Godard, Toronto, Ontario, 1977; the Edmonton Art Gallery, Edmonton, 1977; and Mira Godard, Calgary, 1979.

Tanabe is well known for his portrayals of the prairie and foothills landscape of Alberta. His acrylic on canvas paintings range in size from 50 cm x 61 cm to approximately 155 cm x 245 cm. Tanabe's distinct imagery is recognizable also in his smaller watercolours, drawings, and lithographs. All works emphasize the strong, bold horizontal sweep of the prairies.

Takao Tanabe lives at 4, 103 Banff Avenue, Banff, Alberta.

Title and date The Land 1975
Medium acrylic on canvas
Size 81 cm x 142.5 cm

Lavoine McCullagh

orn in Kitchener, Ontario, in 1945, Lavoine McCullagh graduated from the University of Waterloo, Ontario. She moved to Edmonton in 1967 and began weaving in 1971. McCullagh has taught primitive weaving, four-harness weaving, spinning, and dyeing classes in Edmonton.

Her weavings can be found in the Alberta Art Foundation Collection, Edmonton, and several corporate col-

lections such as R. Angus, Edmonton; Daon Development Corporation, Edmonton; Allarco, Edmonton; and RGO Office Services, Edmonton. She has exhibited through the Downstairs Gallery, Edmonton; West End Gallery, Edmonton; and at the Glenbow-Alberta Institute, Calgary, in the Alberta Art Foundation *Summer '77* show.

During the past year McCullagh has been concerned with exploring basketry techniques as a structural ele-

ment in three-dimensional pieces. She also borrows from stitchery, rug weaving, knitting, and appliqué techniques. Many of McCullagh's works utilize colour graduation in natural tones; however, because she works generally on commissions, colour format and technique are often controlled by the environment in which the weaving will be placed.

McCullagh lives and works at 9530-142 Street, Edmonton, Alberta.

Title and date untitled 1977
Medium wool
Size 90 cm x 153 cm

J.P.Nourry-Barry

J P. Nourry-Barry was born in Kingston, Ontario, in 1927. She studied at Queen's University, Kingston, Ontario, and the University of Alberta, Edmonton. Nourry-Barry recently completed a book of poetry entitled *Boy o Ho-Bo,* with illustrated reproductions of her drawings and sculpture.

Her work can be found in the collection of Alberta Housing and Public Works, Edmonton, and private collections in Europe and Canada. Group shows include *Alberta Realists,* the Edmonton Art Gallery, Edmonton, 1974; *Alberta Summer Show,* the Edmonton Art Gallery, Edmonton, 1974; *For An Independent Hairy Hill,* the Edmonton Art Gallery, Edmonton, 1974; the *National Gallery Travelling Exhibition,* 1974; and *Three Painters,* Latitude 53 Gallery, Edmonton, 1975.

Although her writing and her art work are separate entities, they have a basic interdependence. For the past several years she has experimented with pointillism in acrylic on canvas. Her more recent works are watercolour and ink on paper. These are landscape based and are often painted out of doors. She is also involved with sculpting, both figurative and non-figurative, usually in ciment fondue.

J.P. Nourry-Barry lives at Box 6, Site 16, R.R.2, Sherwood Park, Alberta.

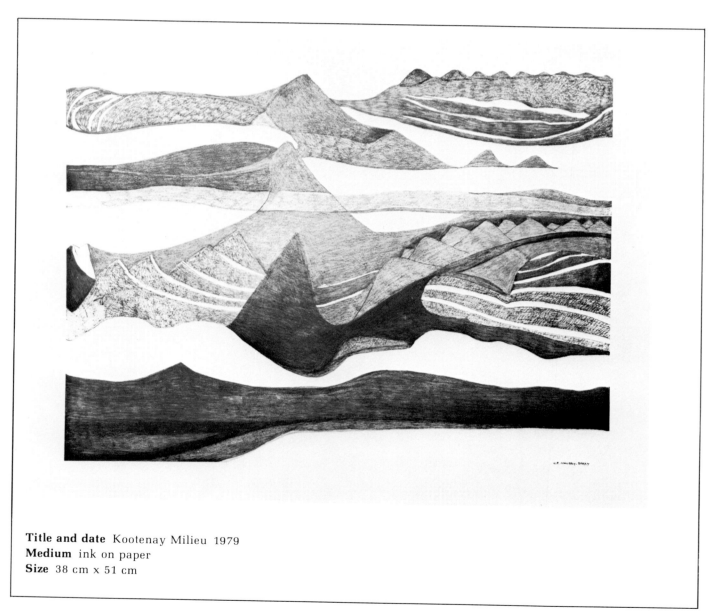

Title and date Kootenay Milieu 1979
Medium ink on paper
Size 38 cm x 51 cm

Cornelius Martens

Cornelius Martens was born in the Ukraine, USSR, 1918. He has been a resident of Alberta for over forty years. Martens is a self-taught professional artist.

His sculpture is contained in the Alberta Art Foundation Collection, Edmonton; Alberta House, London, England; and the Riveredge Foundation, Calgary. Martens exhibits within the province, and his work is on display and sold through his home in Coaldale, Alberta.

Martens sculpts in bronze exclusively. He does his own casting in Coaldale, Alberta. Martens creates bronzes of the modern west—cowboys wearing wrist-watches, beads, and long hair.

"These cowboys are available to me as models at any time. There was a great change in the last twenty years, and in all likelihood there will be a change in the next twenty. To me, it's important to preserve what we have now."

Martens can be reached through the mail at Box 166, Coaldale, Alberta.

Title and date Two Rivers: Colonel MacLeod and Jerry Potts 1973
Medium bronze
Size 42 cm x 23 cm x 30 cm

Stanford Perrott

Stanford Perrott was born in Claresholm, Alberta, in 1917. He graduated from the Alberta College of Art, Calgary, and attended the Banff Centre School of Fine Arts, Banff; the Hans Hofmann School of Fine Art, New York; Art Students League, New York; and Atelier 17, New York. He has served on the Art Advisory Committee of Red Deer College, Red Deer, Alberta, and the Exhibition Committee of Mount Royal College, Calgary. Perrott was a member of the original Alberta Visual Arts Board; a Senator of the University of Calgary, 1971 to 1974; and on the Search Committee of the Alberta Art Foundation, Edmonton, between 1974 and 1976.

His awards include Government of Alberta Achievement Award for Service in Art Education and an honorary membership in the Alberta Society of Artists. Perrott's work is housed in the University of Calgary Permanent Collection and the Glenbow-Alberta Institute, Calgary, as well as in private collections. Perrott has held one-man shows at the Calgary Allied Arts Centre, Calgary; Focus Gallery, Edmonton; and Mount Royal College Art Gallery, Calgary, 1977. He has participated in group exhibitions across Canada.

Perrott paints in watercolour because of its gentle, colourful transparency and its unpredictable qualities, which insist on technical control. His present preoccupation with landscape "represents an unsophisticated attempt to experience and share the pleasure of escape into an idealized, sometimes romantic countryside. Images bear a minimum abstraction relative to modern modes in anticipation that there will be fewer impediments to the viewer's finding his own level and range of appreciation when reacting to each painting."

Stanford Perrott lives at Box 207, Bragg Creek, Alberta.

Title and date Limber Pines, Lundbreck Trussels 1977
Medium watercolour
Size 52 cm x 72 cm

Maureen Enns

Born in Chilliwack, British Columbia, in 1943, Maureen Enns received a Bachelor of Education from the University of British Columbia, Vancouver, in 1965 and a Master of Education from the University of Calgary in 1971. She is currently an instructor at the Alberta College of Art, Calgary.

Enns has received many awards, including the Manisphere Painting Award, Winnipeg, Manitoba, 1974, and a Canada Council grant in 1975, 1977, and 1979. Her paintings may be found in the Convention Center, Calgary; the Law Courts Building, Edmonton; the Alberta Art Foundation, Edmonton; Jubilee Auditorium, Edmonton; and numerous corporate and private collections in Western Canada. Since 1970 Enns has participated in many group shows throughout the western provinces. She was represented in *West '71*, the Edmonton Art Gallery, Edmonton, 1971; *Manisphere*, the Winnipeg Art Gallery, Winnipeg, Manitoba, 1974; the *Alberta Art Foundation Premiere Exhibition*, 1975-76; *What's New*, the Edmonton Art Gallery, Edmonton, 1976; and *Spectrum Canada*, cross-Canada touring exhibition, 1976. In 1977 she was selected by the Glenbow Institute to be included in a three-person show which toured Banff, Lethbridge, Calgary, and Spokane. She held a one-person show at Equinox Gallery, Vancouver, 1979.

Maureen Enns's paintings combine both realism and abstraction. She places one area of sky-scape against another or in the middle of another. This suspension of a realistic three-dimensional form against or within a realistic space results in a surrealistic quality. She terms these areas of sky-scape slices of "skytime." Enns paints with acrylic on canvas, and her paintings range in size from 120 cm x 50 cm to 150 cm x 185 cm.

Enns can be contacted at her home and studio at Box 446, Cochrane, Alberta, as well as through the Alberta College of Art, 1301-16 Avenue NW, Calgary, Alberta.

Title and date Sky Hill 1977
Medium acrylic on canvas
Size 121.5 cm x 152 cm

Gary Tucker

ary Tucker was born in Calgary, 1951. He graduated from the Alberta College of Art as a printmaking major, 1974, and he is employed at the Glenbow-Alberta Institute as an installation foreman.

Tucker received an Alberta Cultural Assistance Award while a student, as well as an award for his work in the *Albertawork* juried exhibition, the University of Calgary and the Alberta College of Art, Calgary, 1977. His work can be found in the permanent collections of the University of Alberta, Edmonton; the Alberta College of Art, Calgary; and many private collections.

Group exhibitions include the *Alberta College of Art Graduate Show*, Calgary, 1974; *Mid-Western Manisphere*, travelling juried show, May 1976 to October 1976; *Albertawork*, the University of Calgary and the Alberta College of Art, Calgary, 1977; the *Alberta Society of Artists Annual Exhibition*, 1978; and *Fifteen*, the Walter J. Phillips Gallery, Banff, Alberta, 1979. Tucker mounted a solo show at the Alberta College of Art, Calgary, 1974, and at the University of Calgary, 1979.

Tucker works with oil on canvas and with a mixture of media on paper. His latest paper work combines ink, pastel, charcoal, glue, pencil, and watercolour. All of his works are large, sombre in colour, and flush with the frontal plane. Grotesque characters in combat with each other fill every inch of the composition. They are dramatic and horrifying scenes symbolic of Tucker's interest in "man's basic aggressive tendencies." Tucker has produced painted, three-dimensional ceramic figures which relate closely to his two-dimensional work.

Gary Tucker's home and studio address is 7204 Huntridge Hill NE, Calgary, Alberta.

Title and date An Unlikely Encounter 1977
Medium mixed media on paper
Size 111.5 cm x 192.5 cm

Lylian Klimek

Lylian Klimek was born in Humboldt, Saskatchewan, 1942. She received a Master of Visual Arts in sculpture from the University of Alberta, Edmonton, 1975, after having completed the requirements for a Bachelor of Fine Arts in sculpture, 1973, and a Master of Sociology, 1968. She is presently a full-time instructor of sculpture at the Alberta College of Art, Calgary.

Permanent collections containing Klimek's work are the Alberta Art Foundation, Edmonton; the University of Alberta, Edmonton; and Government House, Edmonton. She has participated in several group shows since 1972. She was represented in *Woman as Viewer*, the Winnipeg Art Gallery, Winnipeg, 1975, and has held one-person shows at the Hole-in-the-Wall Gallery, Edmonton, 1975, and Latitude 53 Gallery, Edmonton, 1978.

Klimek's main concern is with externalizing her personal response to the mystery and vitality of forms found in nature and to communicate this sense of vitality to the viewer. She experiments with a variety of media, including fibreglass, concrete, paper pulp, and wood, and tries to incorporate the natural properties of these materials into the imagery. As traditional sculpting techniques do not always produce the qualities she searches for, Klimek experiments with forming techniques (casting and assembling) as well. She feels that the experiments themselves are an important facet of her work.

Klimek can be reached through the Alberta College of Art, 1301-16 Avenue NW, Calgary, Alberta, or at her home address of 2106-18A Street NW, Calgary, Alberta.

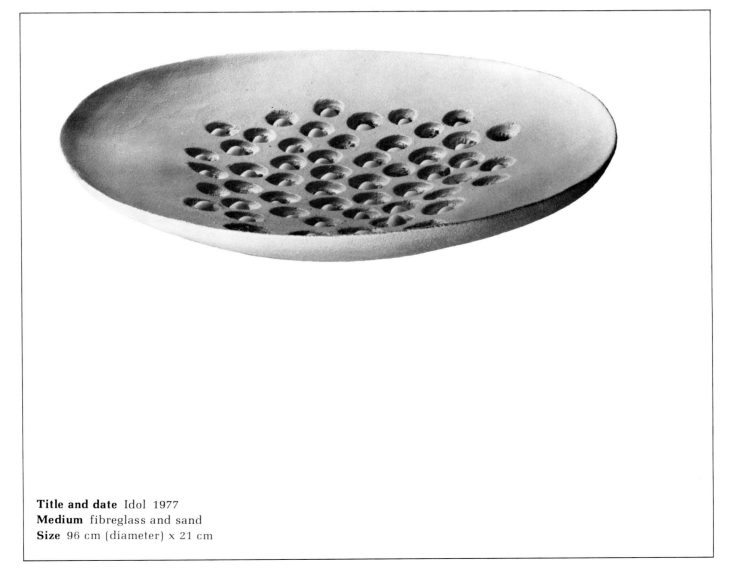

Title and date Idol 1977
Medium fibreglass and sand
Size 96 cm (diameter) x 21 cm

Harry Kiyooka

Harry Kiyooka was born in Calgary in 1928. He has studied extensively and received a Bachelor of Education from the University of Alberta, Edmonton, followed by a Bachelor of Fine Arts from the University of Manitoba. He received a Master of Arts from Michigan State University in 1956 and a Master of Fine Arts from the University of Colorado in 1957. He continued his studies for three years in Italy, and on his return to Canada in 1961 he accepted a teaching position at the University of Calgary, Calgary, where he is an instructor of painting and drawing.

Kiyooka was awarded Canada Council scholarships in 1959 and 1960; Jacox Award—Joint Prize, Edmonton, 1965; First Prize in Painting, *Winnipeg Biennial*, Winnipeg Art Gallery, Winnipeg, Manitoba, 1966; as well as several purchase prizes. Collections containing Kiyooka's work are the Alberta Art Foundation, Edmonton; the Winnipeg Art Gallery, Winnipeg, Manitoba; the Canada Council Art Bank, Ottawa, Ontario; the Edmonton Art Gallery, Edmonton; and the Universities of Victoria, British Columbia, and Calgary. Kiyooka's exhibitions include *Exposition Internationales de Gravure*, Ljubljana, Yugoslavia, 1971, 1973, 1975; *Third Exposition Internationale de Gravure*, Frechen, Germany, 1975; *Spectrum Canada*, Montreal, Quebec, 1976; *Albertawork*, Alberta College of Art and the University of Calgary, Calgary, 1977; and *Canadian Hardedge Art*, Amsterdam, Holland, 1977. A one-person exhibition covering twenty-five years of work was held at the Alberta College of Art, Calgary, January-February, 1978.

For the last eight years Kiyooka has been working on a series of acrylic paintings titled *The Aegean Series*, which reflects his interest in Greek and Roman Art. His canvases are monumental in size, with dimensions of 213.5 cm x 213.5 cm. As well as painting he also experiments with pen and ink, charcoal, and various other mixed media on paper. Kiyooka's work in printmaking has been predominantly with silk-screen, and he employs such reproduction processes as photographs, direct transfers, and hand-cut stencils.

His studio address is Box 10, Site 27, R.R. 2, Calgary, Alberta.

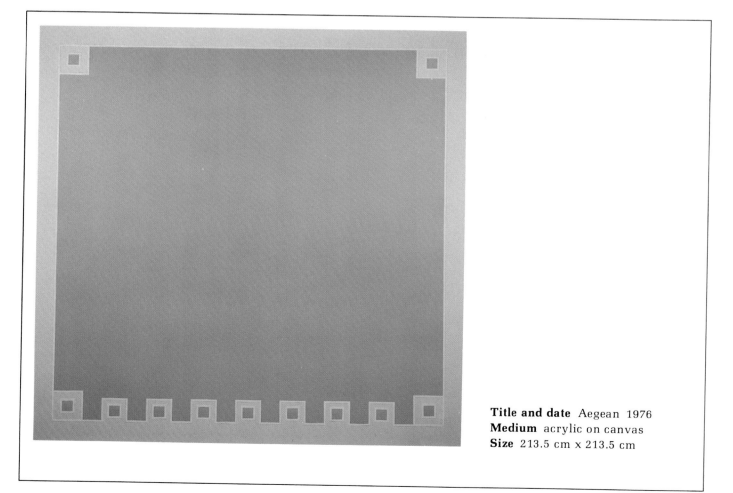

Title and date Aegean 1976
Medium acrylic on canvas
Size 213.5 cm x 213.5 cm

Robert Sinclair

Robert Sinclair was born in Saltcoats, Saskatchewan, in 1939. He received a Bachelor of Fine Arts from the University of Manitoba, Winnipeg, Manitoba, in 1962, as well as a Master of Arts, 1965, and a Master of Fine Arts, 1967, from the University of Iowa, Iowa City, Iowa. Sinclair has held teaching positions at the University of Iowa and the Department of Art and Design, the University of Alberta, Edmonton, where he is an instructor of painting.

Some of the many permanent collections housing Sinclair's work are the Canada Council Art Bank, Ottawa, Ontario; Toronto Dominion Bank Collection, Toronto, Ontario; the Fathers of Confederation Gallery, Charlottetown, Prince Edward Island; the Alberta Art Foundation, Edmonton; and several universities across Canada. Since 1965 Robert Sinclair has held at least one solo exhibition a year at galleries such as Chapman Galleries, Red Deer, 1977; Equinox Gallery, Vancouver, British Columbia, 1978; and Aggregation Gallery, Toronto, Ontario, 1979. Principal group exhibitions include *New Acquisitions*, Confederation Centre Art Gallery, Charlottetown, Prince Edward Island, 1977; the *53rd Annual Exhibition of the Canadian Society of Painters in Watercolor*, New Brunswick Museum, St. John, New Brunswick, 1978; *The Challenge of Watercolour and Landscape*, Southern Ontario circulating tour, 1978 to 1980; and the *Elizabeth Greenshields Award Winners Exhibition*, Canada House, London, England, 1979-80.

Sinclair paints watercolour on paper and acrylic stain on raw cotton. In both the watercolour and the acrylic stain paintings the initial image is developed first through line and later through the application of colour. Subject matter can be divided into two major themes—growing plant life and the road in landscape. Sinclair also utilizes the road in landscape theme in his plexi-glass sculpture. These are constructed from a single sheet of plexi-glass which is heated and hand bent. Colour is applied by airbrush, and the edges of the plexi-glass are polished, functioning as a three-dimensional line. The unpainted areas play a major role in the composition of both the paintings and the sculptures.

The mailing address for Sinclair's home and studio is 1-18, R.R.2, Winterburn, Alberta.

Title and date Mountain Show 1976
Medium watercolour on paper
Size 21.5 cm x 17 cm

Nancy Dodds

A graduate from the Alberta College of Art, Calgary, Nancy Dodds was born in High River in 1953. She studied for a year in Toronto, Ontario, 1978-79.

Dodds received Alberta Cultural Assistance Grants for continuing study in 1976, 1977, and 1978. Her work can be found in the permanent collection of the Alberta College of Art, Calgary. Since her graduation from the Alberta College of Art, Calgary, in 1976, Dodds has worked for the Calgary Separate School Board as an instructional assistant for the Fine Arts Centre, Calgary. Exhibits include the *Graduate Show*, the Alberta College of Art, Calgary, and the *Stampede Art Exhibit*, Calgary, 1977.

Nancy Dodds is primarily interested in experimenting with fibre, generally paper and cloth. She has been involved with the paper making process and the craft of book binding for the last few years. Dodds also produces prints, mostly embossed works, for their subtle gradients of dark and light, and photocopied transfers which are applied to the surface of both paper and cloth. Her work deals mainly with the exploration of different tactile properties of materials which can be overlaid and stitched together.

Mail will be forwarded to Dodds through 123 Lake Arrow Green SE, Calgary, Alberta.

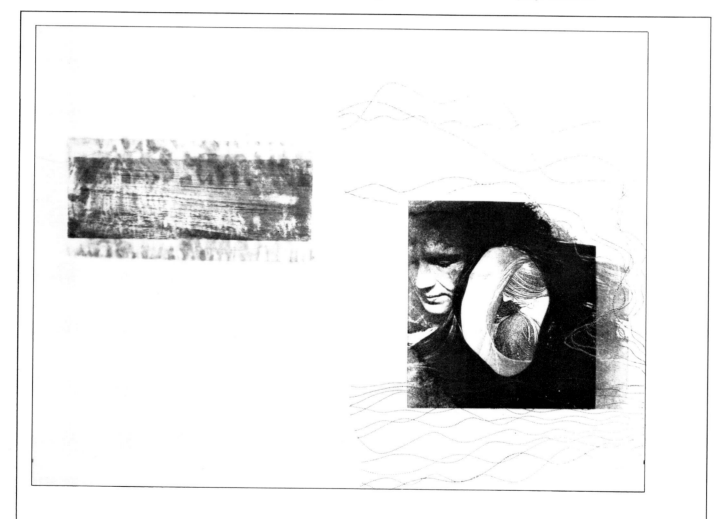

Title and date Waves of Though 1977
Medium mixed media, including colour photocopy
Size 49 cm x 60.5 cm

John Snow

John Snow was born in Vancouver, British Columbia, in 1911. He studied life drawing under Maxwell Bates between 1947 and 1949 and became interested in lithography after visiting Glen Alps at the University of Washington.

Awards include honourable mention at the Salon Des Beaux Arts, Paris, France, 1965; a Canada Council grant, 1966; purchase award, the *Vancouver Print International*, 1967; and Medaglia & Diploma di Segnalzione International, Galleria D'Arte Moderna, Ancona, Italy, 1968. Snow is represented in many personal and corporate collections as well as in the Victoria and Albert Museum, London, England; the National Gallery of Canada, Ottawa, Ontario; the Canada Council Art Bank, Ottawa, Ontario; CHAR International, Puerto Rico; Royal Ontario Museum, Toronto, Ontario; the Alberta Art Foundation, Edmonton; and civic and university galleries across Canada. Snow has held many one-person exhibitions across Canada, including the Bau-Xi, Victoria, British Columbia, 1975; Studio Shop and Gallery, West Vancouver, British Columbia, 1975; Attic Gallery, Regina, Saskatchewan, 1976; Lefebvre Galleries, Edmonton, 1976; and Gallery Pascal, Toronto, Ontario, 1978. Recent group exhibitions in which he participated are the *Society of Canadian Painters, Etchers, and Engravers*, at the Commonwealth Institute, London, England, 1974; Salon Des Beaux Arts, Paris, France, 1975; the *Alberta Art Foundation Premiere Exhibition*, European travelling tour, 1975; and *Canadian Printmakers*, Robert Sgueri Gallery, Buffalo, New York, 1975.

In 1972 Snow retired from the Royal Bank of Canada where he had been employed since 1928. He now devotes his time entirely to his art and works in lithography, sculpture, and various painting media. His imagery includes figure studies, still life, and landscape. Colour is of prime importance to him, and his lithographs may be composed of five to eight colours. Snow's sculpture is constructed of cement or ciment fondu over a wire form or shell.

John Snow lives at 915-18 Avenue SW, Calgary, Alberta.

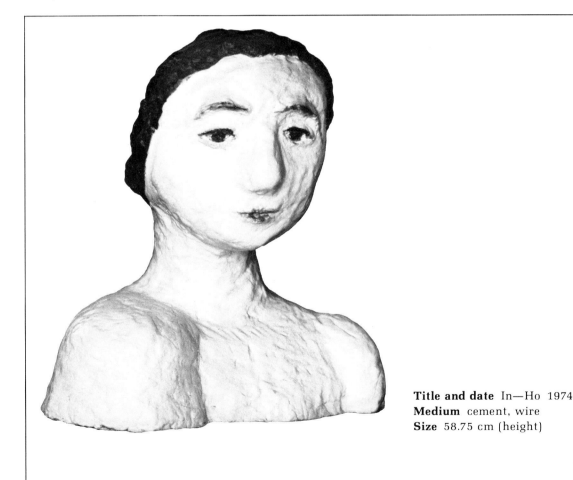

Title and date In—Ho 1974
Medium cement, wire
Size 58.75 cm (height)

Wendy Toogood

Wendy Toogood was born in Bristol, England, in 1947. She graduated from the Alberta College of Art in 1969 and received a tuition scholarship for post-graduate studies at the Instituto Allende, Mexico, 1970. She has been instructing in fabric arts since 1970 and has held workshops across Canada. She is employed with the Fabrics Department at the Alberta College of Art, Calgary.

Toogood has received many awards, including short-term grants from the Canada Council in 1970 and 1973, as well as the prize for excellence at the *Canadian Guild of Crafts Exhibition*, Toronto, Ontario, in 1971, 1972, and 1973; Canada Council Arts Bursary, 1972-73; and the Cultural Assistance Major Award Grant, Government of the Province of Alberta, Department of Culture, 1974. Toogood's work is represented in the Government of Alberta, Edmonton; the Alberta Art Foundation Collection, Edmonton; the Universities of Calgary and Manitoba; the Ontario Institute for Studies in Education Collection, Toronto, Ontario; the Confederation Art Gallery and Museum, Charlottetown, Prince Edward Island; and the Art Gallery of Ontario, Toronto, Ontario. Toogood has held several solo exhibitions since 1971 at such centres as Gallery 111, the University of Manitoba, Winnipeg, Manitoba, 1974, and the University of Calgary, Little Gallery, Calgary, Alberta, 1975. She has also shown in two-person exhibitions across Canada and in such group exhibitions as *Woman As Viewer*, Winnipeg Art Gallery, Winnipeg, Manitoba, 1975; *The Mask Show*, Mildura, Australia, 1976; *Mostly Smaller Works*, Clouds & Water Gallery, Calgary, 1978; and *Bookworks*, Powerhouse, Montreal, Quebec, 1979.

Toogood hand stitches and quilts together an extensive variety of gathered materials in each piece. She explores the visual densities of textiles such as opaque cottons, transparent nylons, and silks and contrasts the different tactile properties of fabrics such as satin and felt, wool and silk. The result is a composition of vibrant colour and intricate imagery.

Toogood can be reached care of the Alberta College of Art, 1301-16 Avenue NW, Calgary, Alberta.

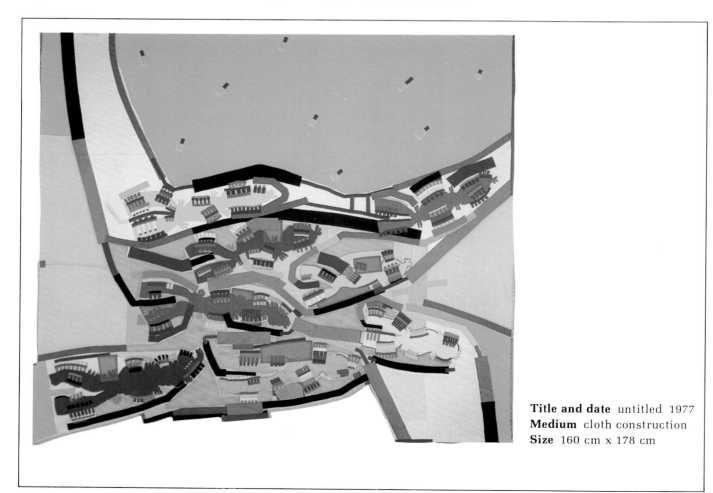

Title and date untitled 1977
Medium cloth construction
Size 160 cm x 178 cm

Lyndal Osborne

Lyndal Osborne was born in Newcastle, New South Wales, Australia, in 1940. She received a Bachelor of Arts from the National Art School, Sydney, Australia, 1960, and a Master of Fine Arts from the University of Wisconsin, Madison, Wisconsin, 1971. Osborne has been a printmaking instructor with the Department of Art and Design, University of Alberta, Edmonton, since 1971. She has also taught at the University of Wisconsin and at the University of Houston in Houston, Texas.

Scholarships and awards include the first class prize from the *International Exhibition of Children's Work* held at Asnieres, Paris, France, 1956; the National Art School Scholarship, 1958; the New South Wales Teachers' College Scholarship, 1959 through 1961; a Canada Council Travel Grant, 1976; and a grant from Advanced Education and Manpower, Government of Alberta, to assist in a joint print-making exhibition with Osaka University of Arts, Japan, and the University of Alberta, Edmonton. Osborne's work can be found in the permanent collections of several corporations and art institutes in North America, some of which are the Art Bank of Canada, Ottawa, Ontario; the National Gallery, Ottawa, Ontario; University of Milwaukee Union, Milwaukee, Wisconsin; the Burnaby Art Gallery, Vancouver, British Columbia; and Government House, Edmonton. Osborne has also participated in over one-hundred group exhibitions since 1968; the most recent are the *6th International Biennale of Printmaking*, Krakow, Poland, 1976; the *California Society of Printmakers Travelling Exhibit*, 1977; *Selections, Alberta Art Foundation*, the Glenbow-Alberta Institute, Calgary, Alberta, 1977; *Graphex 5* and *6*, Annual Juried Exhibition of Canadian Prints and Drawings, Brantford, Ontario, 1977 and 1978; the *Print and Drawing Council of Canada's Non-Juried Exhibition of Small Prints and Drawings*, University of Calgary, Calgary, Alberta, 1977; *Alberta Artists*, Artcore Gallery, Vancouver, 1978.

For the past five years Osborne has been working on large airbrushed drawings, as well as printmaking. In printmaking the scale of her work is often dictated by the pressbed size, but in the drawings she is able to extend the dimensions of her work. Airbrush technique has also allowed Osborne a more direct and spontaneous approach to the work. Subject matter is a selection of natural and man-made objects such as mushrooms, flowers, buns, and jujubes, which she manipulates in groups within a special environment. She is familiar with all printmaking media; however, most prints are silk-screen and lithography combinations.

Lyndal Osborne lives at 10738-123 Street, Edmonton, Alberta.

Title and date Reaching Out 1977
Medium airbrush drawing
Size 97 cm x 106.5 cm

Title page painting—*Grace* by John Hall

The art work in *Artists of Alberta* was photographed by Chris Newell, Ranson
Photographers Limited, with the following exceptions:
Impartial Observer—photograph by Ron Berglund
Missing the Ten Spot is Indicative of One's Life—photograph by Dennis Evans
Untitled by Christina Greco—photograph courtesy of the artist
Late in the Day—photograph by Ron Berglund
Friendship—photograph courtesy of the artist
Structured Relief Triptych—photograph courtesy of the artist
July—photograph courtesy of the artist
Untitled by Clyde McConnell—photograph courtesy of the artist
Kootenay Milieu—photograph by Lauren Dale
Twist & Flip—photograph courtesy of the artist
Hair—photograph by Jim Dow
Untitled by John Roberts—photograph courtesy of the artist
Venetian Puddle—photograph courtesy of the artist
Landspace Twenty-One—photograph courtesy of the artist
Matrimony—photograph courtesy of the Alberta Art Foundation

John Hall's *Grace* is in the Calgary Civic Collection
Douglas Motter's *This Bright Hand* is in the collection of the Calgary Convention Center
James McLaren Nicoll's *Steam* is in the collection of the Alberta Art Foundation
Marion Nicoll's *Runes B* is in the collection of the Alberta Art Foundation

Artists of Alberta has been published with the assistance of the following contributors:
Pitfield Mackay Ross and Company Limited, Calgary
Builders Contract Management, Edmonton
Mr. and Mrs. A. M. Millard, Calgary
Mr. H. A. Walcot, Calgary
Cotswold Art Consultants Limited, Edmonton
Canada Council
Advanced Education and Manpower, The Government of Alberta